The Best

NIKOLAUS PEVSNER

Buildings of England

AN ANTHOLOGY BY BRIDGET CHERRY AND JOHN NEWMAN

WITH AN INTRODUCTION BY JOHN NEWMAN

VIKING

VIKING

Penguin Books Ltd, Harmondsworth, Middlesex, England
Viking Penguin Inc., 40 West 23rd Street, New York, New York 10010, U.S.A.
Penguin Books Australia Ltd, Ringwood, Victoria, Australia
Penguin Books Canada Limited, 2801 John Street, Markham, Ontario, Canada L3R 1B4
Penguin Books (N.Z.) Ltd, 182–190 Wairau Road, Auckland 10, New Zealand

The extracts that comprise this selection appeared first
in the volumes of the Buildings of England series listed on page 232.
This selection first published 1986

Typeset in Monophoto Sabon
Printed in Great Britain by Wm. Clowes Ltd, Beccles and London

British Library Cataloguing in Publication Data
Pevsner, Nikolaus
   The best buildings of England.
   1. Architecture—England
   I. Title   II. Cherry, Bridget III. Newman,
   John, 1936–
   720'. 942 NA 961

ISBN 0-670-81283-8
Designed by Cinamon and Kitzinger

Contents

7 Preface

9 Introduction

26 Anglo-Saxon: seventh to eleventh centuries

32 Norman Churches and Monasteries: late eleventh to late twelfth centuries

44 Norman Military Architecture

48 Early English Gothic: late twelfth to late thirteenth centuries

62 Decorated Gothic: late thirteenth to mid fourteenth centuries

78 Perpendicular Gothic: mid fourteenth to early sixteenth centuries

90 Secular Architecture from the late thirteenth to the early sixteenth century

104 Architecture and Sculpture of the mid sixteenth century

112 Elizabethan and Jacobean Architecture: 1560–1620

122 Mature Classicism: 1620–1700

134 English Baroque: 1700–1735

142 Palladian and Gothick: 1715–1775

152 Neo-classicism: 1760–1820

164 Post-Reformation Monuments

174 The Picturesque: 1800–1850

180 Early Victorian Churches

186 High Victorian: 1850–1885

202 Arts and Crafts: 1885–1900

210 Edwardian: 1901–1914

216 Modern: 1930–1965

228 Acknowledgements for Photographs

229 Index

232 Complete List of *The Buildings of England* Titles

THUS DID NOAH ACCORDING TO ALL THAT GOD COMMANDED HIM

Preface

The stimulus to publish this book has been provided by the Pevsner Memorial Trust, set up in 1986 to raise money to rescue and conserve an important work of art in an English building in memory of Sir Nikolaus Pevsner. The work chosen is the scheme of wall paintings executed in 1865 by Clayton & Bell under G. E. Street's supervision in the church of St Michael, Garton-on-the-Wolds, Humberside. A detail of the wall paintings is illustrated opposite. Pevsner's reaction on seeing them in 1970 was: 'It is essential that they be preserved' (*Yorkshire: York and the East Riding*). In the succeeding years they have deteriorated further, so a substantial sum of money is needed to conserve them. The target figure is £100,000. A proportion of royalties from the sale of this book will go to the Appeal, and those who wish to make personal donations are requested to send cheques to Pevsner Memorial Trust, c/o 36 St Paul's Square, York, YO2 4BD.

Thanks are due to the Pevsner family for giving permission to quote extracts from Sir Nikolaus's books. In choosing suitable passages the editors received prompt help from Edward Hubbard, Alexandra Wedgwood and Elizabeth Williamson. A number of photographers took pictures specially for the book, and we should like to acknowledge their efforts, achieved at speed during a period of inclement weather, by listing their names here: James Austin, Christopher Dalton, Alan Greeley, George Hall, Geoff Howard, Eddie Ryle-Hodges, Colin Westwood and Jeremy Whitaker. Geoffrey Fisher, of the Conway Library, Courtauld Institute of Art, was also a great help. But none of this activity could have been set in motion without the enthusiasm and energy of two members of staff of Penguin, Stephen Davies and Susan Rose-Smith, and to them we offer our hearty thanks. The index was compiled by Judy Nairn, whom we also want to thank for much editorial improvement to the text.

The introduction comes from the pen of one of the editors but incorporates the ideas of them both. The brief editorial passages on each page are intended to link the chosen buildings into a historical sequence. The main passages, however, apart from the necessary minor editorial adaptations, are entirely in the words of Sir Nikolaus Pevsner, and are taken from first editions. In a few places factual corrections have been silently introduced to take account of recent research.

St Michael, Garton-on-the-Wolds, Humberside, the Building of the Ark,
with scenes of the Creation below,
a detail of the wall paintings of 1865 by Clayton & Bell whose restoration
is the aim of the Pevsner Memorial Trust

Introduction

The aim of this book is to present some of the finest architecture and decoration in England as seen through the eyes of one man, the late Sir Nikolaus Pevsner, a tireless traveller and perhaps the best-informed observer ever to devote himself to the study and appreciation of our architectural heritage. For over a quarter of a century, from 1945 to 1974, he produced the volumes of a county-by-county series, *The Buildings of England*, in which he attempted to assess historically and aesthetically every building of architectural interest in the country. In the following pages we reprint from his books the words he wrote about one hundred of them, buildings which for him represented the cream of the cream and which challenged him to respond with the full range of his scholarship and the full fire of his enthusiasm. You may now wish to turn on straight away to enjoy the plates and to savour Pevsner's judgements on the works of art they illustrate. In this introduction I shall try to say something about Pevsner's taste, its formation, its character and influence.

But first a disclaimer. Pevsner set himself a superhuman task. He had intended that the forty-six volumes needed to cover the forty historic English counties (i.e. before the redrawing of county boundaries in 1974, and excluding Monmouthshire) should all be written by himself, at the rate of two a year, each based on a period of four or five weeks during which by day he would travel and look and in the evening, usually in a modest hotel bedroom, write up what he had just seen. In the event, although he carried through this relentless régime almost without a break from 1947 to 1972, between the ages of 45 and 70, he was forced to bring in collaborators to cope with several of the counties, and two he handed over entirely to other authors. So the buildings of Gloucestershire and Kent he did not write about at all, and he entrusted to others almost the whole of Surrey, all Oxfordshire except Oxford itself, half each of Sussex, Lincolnshire, and Dorset, and smaller parts of Warwickshire (i.e. Birmingham), Hampshire, and Cheshire. Pevsner therefore never wrote a full analysis and critique of such transcendently important buildings as the cathedrals of Canterbury and Gloucester, and a number of other scarcely less eligible examples – Tewkesbury Abbey, Blenheim Palace – are perforce excluded from the present anthology.

Even so, in order to bring the number illustrated here down to just over a hundred, some pretty hard choices have had to be made. On the whole longer passages have been selected rather than pithy comments, however telling, because Pevsner was undoubtedly roused by certain buildings to write at unusual length and with special intensity because they seemed to him to express especially clearly or successfully general characteristics to which he wanted to draw attention. So he allowed himself, perhaps a dozen or more times in each county, what amounts to a purple passage, and it is a selection of these which is reprinted here. Nevertheless Pevsner could also use a mere sentence, or even a single word, to say all that needed to be said; of these a few examples have been included.

This anthology aims to celebrate the glories of English architecture, and of painting and sculpture in association with architecture, from the Anglo-Saxon period to as near to the present day as possible – it concludes with a building of 1960 which Pevsner thought 'a perfect piece of architecture'; but within the span Pevsner's own preferences and even prejudices are given weight, and so is his delight in the unfamiliar discovery. A dispassionate balance has not been sought; this is a personal anthology of the best buildings of England.

The rest of this introduction will attempt to explain these preferences and prejudices, and in particular to stress the foundations on which they are laid.

First of all, Pevsner never admitted the defeatist view expressed in the tag *de gustibus non est disputandum*. On the contrary, taste can be trained, and can thereby yield much enhanced enjoyment, both sensual and intellectual, as well as fostering disdain for vulgar displays. 'For the layman,' he remarks in an aside at Much Wenlock Priory (*Shropshire*), 'a training of aesthetic sensibilities and of a historical sense is equally desirable.' The naive enthusiasm of Kelly's Street Directory for a Victorian Gothic church in Cumberland (Cleator, *Cumberland and Westmorland*) provokes a rare outburst of ridicule: 'Rock-faced, with lancets. The bellcote very fanciful in its details and therefore called by Kelly "of exceeding beauty" . . . Very fanciful, very ornate, and exactly what one means by debased in descriptions of Victorian architecture is the interior . . . Kelly's adjectives are "exquisite", "chaste", and "elegant".' Sound aesthetic responses must rest on the ability to make valid comparisons, both formal and historical. Indeed the texts of *The Buildings of England* themselves provide, in a manner that the reader can experience and exploit in whatever way he will, a multi-faceted training in making such comparisons. Pevsner readily quotes the opinions of others: Celia Fiennes, Horace Walpole, Ruskin, Eastlake, and, probably most frequently, H. S. Goodhart-Rendel, connoisseur of Victorian churches. The views of such authors, if just and trenchantly expressed, deserve to be aired. Sometimes Pevsner offers them in disagreement with himself, as at Sledmere (*Yorkshire: East Riding*), where he dismisses Temple Moore's major church of 1897 as 'patently dull' but feels that he should also draw attention to Goodhart-Rendel's conflicting estimate, 'perhaps one of the loveliest churches of England'. 'To such an extent', he remarks, 'can reactions differ.'

Pevsner started with an advantage possessed by no other serious commentator on English architecture: his Continental birth, background, and training. Born in 1902 in Leipzig of Russian Jewish stock, and resident in Germany until he was thirty-three, his first book was an account of Italian Mannerist and Baroque painting. His interest in British art and architecture developed while teaching at Göttingen University in the early 1930s, and when in 1935 the rise of Hitler forced him to leave his native soil for good, it was in London that he settled. In his mind the Continental context was always present, giving detachment and authority to his judgements on the art of his adopted country.

It is probable that Pevsner himself would have attached an even greater significance to the fact that he had been trained as a historian. This found expression in a number of ways. He never tired of the archaeological puzzles presented by medieval parish churches. His practice when confronted by an unfamiliar building for the first time was invariable – and on his travels he might visit between a dozen and twenty parish churches in a day. He would walk round the outside first, noting every feature of interest, whether a finely designed or characteristic window or doorway or merely a tell-tale joint in the masonry which might suggest a break in the building programme or an alteration; then he would go inside and do the same for the interior; and only after that would he get out the notes prepared for him by his research assistant, from which he would discover what had already been published by way of historical documentation or archaeological analysis. Thus by the time he read the interpretations of others he had often made up his own mind about the building's history and development. What he read might confirm his unaided deductions; if on the other hand it challenged him to justify them, a lively and argumentative text was often the result. The unavailability for inspection of so many house interiors and the generally simpler and more obvious constructional history of more recent buildings rendered the analysis of domestic buildings and post-medieval architecture less amenable to this approach.

A highly developed sense of historical styles was one of Pevsner's principal tools of analysis. He could elicit the story of an undocumented building by a visual comparison of the parts with one another and with the stock of forms and motifs which constitute the ingredients of each generic style. Thomas Rickman, the inventor of the terms Early English, Decorated, and Perpendicular for the three principal phases of English Gothic architecture, was one of Pevsner's heroes. He was predisposed to treat style as the visual manifestation of the spirit of the age, in a Germanic way, and relatively uninterested in the interaction of artistic personalities, the means whereby styles did in fact develop and change. In this too his sympathy lay with the Middle Ages and its artistic anonymity rather than, say, with the Georgian period, where personal idiosyncrasies can be studied, but not, as Pevsner felt, to any wider or more significant purpose. Occasional traces can even be found of a cyclical view of art, whereby a style will proceed through the stages of experimental infancy and balanced maturity to senility and collapse, as for instance in his remarks on the crossing tower at Hereford Cathedral: 'It illustrates the change from 1260 to 1310 to perfection, a change from the Greek, i.e. classic, ideal of μηδὲν ἀγάν and the Gothic ideal of *masze*, as Wolfram von Eschenbach glorifies it, to profusion, excesses, and so final exhaustion.'

Pevsner always paid great attention to transitional phases, the moment when one style passed into another – Norman into Gothic, Early English into Decorated – or a new idiom was superimposed, as Renaissance forms came to overlay Gothic in the early sixteenth century. He made an important contribution to the history of classical architecture in England in stressing the role of the Lord Protector Somerset and his circle about 1550 in introducing a more architecturally serious approach to classicism, and in assessing the following century he gave Inigo Jones due credit for his final mastery of the classical idiom and influence in diffusing a new understanding of it through the country.

Pevsner was also fascinated by the phenomenon of historicism, the deliberate revival of past styles. The two interests came together in the Gothic of the seventeenth century. Churches in this style always provoked a comment. His appetite for historicism was a root cause of his interest in Victorian architecture, making him take it seriously, as very few indeed of his contemporaries did. As late as 1967, for example, he felt it necessary to justify his twenty-four lines describing the church at South Tidworth (*Hampshire and the Isle of Wight*), built in 1879–80 by John Johnson, with its 'strikingly high, short sumptuous nave . . . and a yet more sumptuous chancel' with the words, 'Surely a church like this is as valid a monument of architecture as any of the Middle Ages or the C17 or C18.'

One of his most cherished projects was the investigation of the variety of new building types that evolved during the nineteenth century. This found full expression in his last book, the monumental *A History of Building Types* (1976). His awareness of the nuances of style used to express different functions or purposes was highly developed: the cinquecento palazzo style adopted for provincial banks, for example, he dubbed 'confidence-inspiring'. His comments on the famous, and late lamented, Euston Arch, fronting the first of the London railway terminals, are particularly apt for quotation: 'What then made Hardwick [the architect] go all out for the sublime in his Doric display? The answer is no doubt pride in the achievement of the railway line. Here was something as grandiose of its kind as anything the Greeks ever had accomplished. So it deserved the highest rhetoric available, and that was in the 1830s without doubt Doric.'

Pevsner's sympathy and understanding for Victorian architecture developed a great deal over the years during which he was engaged on *The Buildings of England* as he became influenced, if sometimes also puzzled, by the enthusiasms of the young whose eyes he had himself opened.

If Pevsner approached the buildings of England as a trained historian, prepared to analyse and categorize, he was also drawn to them as an enthusiast, eager to experience and share aesthetic pleasure. Such pleasure is registered on virtually every page of every volume in the series. It may be indicated by a single word, or inspire a sentence or a paragraph of explanation. For pleasure to Pevsner is not such a frail and fleeting emotion, or so personal to each individual, that its essence cannot be conveyed in words. A typical expression of Pevsner's admiration runs like this: a gasp of enthusiasm; the cause of it pinpointed and analysed; then the exposition: 'Skipwith has one of the most noble chancels of the East Riding. What endows it with that quality is that the windows, two s, two n, and even the e window, are straight-headed. They are large windows, and the severe enframement is exquisitely contrasted against the finesse of the tracery, tracery still untouched by the licence of the ogee. The motifs are those of 1300, clear and easy to read . . . But we must keep cool and turn to chronology.' And he proceeds to trace the building's history from the Anglo-Saxon period to its Victorian restoration.

At one end of the spectrum is the thrill of awe which Pevsner feels before the very early, as for instance the crypt of Hexham Priory, 'perhaps the most moving monument of medieval Northumberland'; or before the defiantly surviving ruin, say Covehithe church, Suffolk, 'A moving sight with its commanding w tower and its tall, long, majestic walls through which the wind blows from the sea'; or before the massive or sheer, for example the choir of Worcester Cathedral, 'most thrilling in the Lady Chapel bay and the e transept, where verticalism is unchecked'. At the other end is the indulgent amusement engendered by a humble rustic building such as Rushton Spencer church, Staffordshire, 'a dear little church, all on its own in the fields and architecturally hard to take seriously', or by an artless piece of design such, in the same county, as the Roman Catholic church in Newcastle-under-Lyme designed in 1833 by a priest, James Egan: 'The reverend gentleman was not a connoisseur of the Gothic style, but he had the right ideas and created a church which one will always remember, and with an affectionate smile.' But the central pleasure comes from recognizing architectural beauty. Beauty for Pevsner is epitomized, perhaps, by his feeling for Madley church, Herefordshire: 'The most interesting are not always the most beautiful churches. It is lucky if the two coincide. Madley has both a pure, noble, and generous interior and a fascinating building history . . . [The tower] is a beautiful piece, stately and trustworthy, neither slender nor massive . . . All this Dec work makes the church now appear wonderfully light.' The qualities of balance, classicity, and moderation, particularly when coupled with restraint in decoration, and the effective handling of space and light – these are again and again singled out by Pevsner as the wellsprings of architectural beauty.

The opposite qualities can be expected to inspire disgust, as they do for example at Cold Hanworth (*Lincolnshire*), where J. Croft's 'spiky' church of 1863 with, among other things, tracery which is 'a pattern of ill-applied inventiveness' is condemned as 'a showpiece of High Victorian self-confidence at its most horrible'. But even this sort of thing, if done with enough bravado, could bring a smile to Pevsner's face: of E. B. Lamb's equally roguish church of 1850 at Thirkleby (*Yorkshire: North Riding*) he says, 'It is a veritable riot of forms, perverse and mischievous, and one takes a perverse pleasure in it'. Perverse pleasure.

Pevsner provided both the historical framework and the example of his own reactions in order to elicit richer and more valid architectural responses from his readers. But he was constantly aware of the human element in buildings, that they embodied the ambitions, assumptions, and abilities of their creators, the patrons who paid for them as much as the architects who designed them. In his Reith Lectures of 1955, published the following year under the title *The Englishness of English Art*, Pevsner treated works of art as expressions of traits of national character, and the general approach of these lectures can be found reflected in many of his analyses in *The Buildings of England*. Here are two examples, the first from *Bedfordshire and the County of Huntingdon and Peterborough*, the second from *Yorkshire: The North Riding*. 'Southill is one of the most exquisite English understatements. That so refined and reticent a house could be demanded in 1795 by a brewer is a telling illustration of the rarely admitted cultural possibilities of the Industrial Revolution of the Georgian Era.' And the 'wondrous' Grand Hotel, Scarborough, is 'a High Victorian gesture of assertion and confidence, of denial of frivolity and insistence on substance than which none more telling can be found in the land.' The connection is not always made so openly, but can often nonetheless be sensed. The rash of church building in late medieval Norfolk is connected by Pevsner with the prosperity of the East Anglian wool merchants, which led not only to, say, the four Burnhams with their churches all within a square mile of each other, but to the erection of mighty church towers, such as that at Winterton, 'the work of some donor filled with the *hubris* of prosperous Norfolk merchants in the c 15'. And this overweening quality is surely found by Pevsner, though he does not say so in so many words, in another, much more celebrated, Norfolk tower, that of St Peter Mancroft, Norwich, analysed in purely aesthetic terms: 'The tower, it must be reluctantly admitted, is more rich than aesthetically successful. Every motif has been lavished on it, and in the end this very prodigality has defeated its object.'

If he discerned one, Pevsner would try to put his finger on the precise relationship between the personality of a patron and the character of a building, as in his remarkable characterization of Tattershall church (*Lincolnshire*), built by Ralph Cromwell, Treasurer of England in the mid fifteenth century: 'He was a tenacious man with a great gift for administration, a tidy mind, a faith in accurate records, and an ability to steer a safe course amid the intrigues of the age of Henry VI.' His church, begun in 1440, 'was evidently built regardless of expense and for a man who wanted size rather than pretty decoration. It is in fact almost gaunt in its absence of ornament – to the extent of all windows being left without cusping. The difference this makes to the general impression will be admitted by anyone who has noticed this detail. Another equally telling detail is the liking for triangles instead of arches . . . The whole church is truly what is often said of Perp churches: a glass-house. The interior is consequently, and of course especially because little stained glass remains, extremely light, too light perhaps for any *Stimmung*. One walks through it and stays in it and never quite forgets the Treasurer's badge, which is a purse.'

Of the more conventional view, that buildings epitomize the attitudes of their architects, Pevsner made perhaps less creative use. But there are plenty of examples if one looks for them: 'It is, as it is by Hawksmoor, an excessively grave and pretentious building for its purpose' (Clarendon Building, Oxford). Or, still in Oxford, H. T. Hare's

Town Hall of 1893–7: 'Large and unashamedly showy. Hare gave Oxford town what T. G. Jackson for fifteen years had given Oxford gown. There are the alternately blocked columns, the transomed windows with arched lights, the gables *à la* Kirby. Did Jackson chuckle or foam?' Or even this, on Temple Moore's church of East Moors (*Yorkshire: North Riding*), 1882: 'The young architect obviously enjoyed this job thoroughly, and his pleasure is infectious after eighty years.'

But buildings are not just works of art created by the inner urges of architects in order to satisfy the ambitions of their patrons and the desire of the educated tourist for aesthetic pleasure. They are meant for use, and in considering the value and success of most, but not necessarily all, buildings one must consider their effect on those who inhabit, enter, or pass by them day by day. Naturally this aspect cannot be investigated systematically in a series such as *The Buildings of England*, but Pevsner does make relevant comments, especially if his own 'detached' appreciation is patently inconsistent with the experience of 'users'. T. G. Jackson's operatic Examination Schools were something novel in Victorian Gothic Oxford and they impressed Pevsner mightily, but he does not leave them without remarking, 'What an image of examination such a building creates: the puny candidates and the moloch of the testing machinery.' Contemporary buildings Pevsner naturally tended to view more frequently in this light. At G. G. Pace's church of 1964 in Wythenshawe, Manchester (*South Lancashire*), he wrote: 'All praise to the clients who were willing to accept so daring a design. Much praise to the architect who had the daring to submit so uncompromisingly 1960s a design. And apologies from the author of this volume who cannot appreciate for worship so aggressive a building.' 'For worship' is the key. To a dispassionate observer such as Pevsner, Arup Associates' seventeen-storey tower block at Bracknell (*Berkshire*) is an outstandingly fine building, but, 'rising as it does in lonely splendour, it cudgels down the whole scale of Bracknell'. His conclusion, however, may surprise the present-day reader, twenty years on: 'It calls for four or five more of identical design. They could then create their own environment.'

With this last judgement we are ready to consider Pevsner's personal taste. Naturally, his own particular interests and beliefs led him to be especially sensitive to certain types of buildings and architectural effects and relatively less alert to others.

His Corbusian vision at Bracknell may lead first to a consideration of his attitudes to modern architecture. Pevsner's first book in English, *Pioneers of the Modern Movement from William Morris to Walter Gropius*, published in 1936, twice revised subsequently, and frequently referred to by its author with parental affection as 'My Pioneers', gives the clue to his attitude to the architecture of the twentieth century. He believed that, by starting from function and the nature of materials and by abandoning all styles of the past, Continental architects and designers had by about 1910 managed to formulate a system which was potentially of timeless validity. He watched with the keenest interest the at first dilatory but, after 1945, quickening spread through England of the international modern style. The unassuming quality of such humanly-scaled post-war buildings as the Hertfordshire primary schools and the council estates in Norfolk villages of Tayler & Green especially delighted him. The inherent anonymity of such buildings was for Pevsner a virtue, 'without personality cult' becoming for him a term of praise in modern architecture. He was convinced that there was nothing alien about such an idiom, and when larger and more ambitious buildings began going up in the 1950s he was anxious to publicize examples which had been successfully integrated with buildings of earlier periods.

Once this architectural possibility had been established, he condemned all historicist clinging to past styles, whether the stripped classicism which still lingered for public buildings even into the 1950s, or Gothic for ecclesiastical contexts, or indeed Modernism itself when adopted merely as a style. Here he is, firing a left and right, in Great Marlborough Street in the West End of London: 'At the w end the thoughtful traveller will stop and consider which of two evils of our present civilization he may be readier to put up with. On the l. is Palladium (formerly Ideal) House, an architectural parallel to the Wurlitzer in music – black sheer granite and rich gilt with the lush floral motifs of the Paris Exhibition of 1925 . . . On the r. however is Liberty's Tudor store, 1924 by *Hall*, half-timber and all. The timbers are the real article; they come from genuine men-of-war; they are not just stuck on . . . So technically there is nothing wrong – but functionally and intellectually everything. The scale is wrong, the symmetry is wrong, the proximity to a classical façade put up by the same firm at about the same time is wrong, and the goings-on of a store behind such a façade . . . are wrongest of all.' By contrast, he gives us his vision of modern and medieval harmoniously combined in expressing his disappointment at Great Yarmouth (*North East Norfolk*) where the church of St Nicholas, gutted in 1942, had been rebuilt by an architect who had tried 'to make up his own Transitional and Gothic. What an opportunity was lost thereby! What thrilling things might have been done inside! A modern interior, airy, noble, of fine materials could have arisen to affirm the vitality of C20 church architecture inside the c13 walls. How defeatist does the imitation-Gothic interior appear, once this has been realized.'

The reality of much modern architecture was inevitably disillusioning. Already by 1969, in Manchester (*South Lancashire*) not Bracknell, the limitations of tower blocks were obvious: 'Do we really want these towers of flats everywhere? Do tenants want them? Should they be accepted as living conditions by any but bachelors, spinsters, young couples without children, and old people? Will they not be the slums of fifty years hence?'

Brutalism and other forms of Expressionism which invaded British architecture in the 1960s disillusioned him too. He disapproved of what he saw as self-indulgence by architects, but even more of what appeared to him to be a return to historicism, and dubbed the new generation of architects the 'Anti-Pioneers'. Here one must admit that his attitude was not entirely consistent, for while he could accept the 'brutalism' of Hawksmoor and the over-emphatic massiveness of extreme neo-classicism, he could not, it seems, accept their twentieth-century equivalents. And when his guard was down he was able to appreciate something so obviously Brutalist as William Whitfield's extension to the Institute of Chartered Accountants of 1964–70 (*London I*, 3rd edition): 'Mr Whitfield has done it brilliantly, first by continuing to the corner of Copthall Avenue what had been done in 1930, . . . and then suddenly appearing himself with a short, high, powerful stretch, the concrete surfaces heavily reeded, a windowless staircase expressed by its very steps showing. Here is proof, if proof is needed, that the uncompromisingly new can go with the old, if handled by an appreciative and imaginative architect.' Because William Whitfield had successfully made the juxtaposition he so often pleaded for, he could here accept the Brutalist Whitfield 'himself'.

It is not fair, however, to brand Pevsner's attitude to modern architecture as inconsistent. He championed Gropius, the early Le Corbusier and their intelligent followers because he believed that they were concerned not with the pattern-making, the surface effects, the associationism which a preoccupation with 'style' involves, but, like their medieval and Baroque forerunners, with something which his German background made him consider much more important and fundamental: the effective handling and control of space. The influence of Paul Frankl was probably particularly potent in this respect. The success of the Royal Festival Hall, opened in 1951, 'the first major public building in inner London [and he could have said in Britain] designed in the contemporary style of architecture', must have confirmed him in his view. As he justly comments on this building: 'Aesthetically the greatest achievement, and one which is without doubt internationally remarkable, is the management of inner space.' For an architecture of this sort ornament was an irrelevancy; the supreme virtue was the appropriate – and wherever possible the dramatic and uplifting – expression of the fundamental purpose of all architecture, the enclosure of space. In practice, however, he recognized that ornamentalism could never be kept at bay for long. He spotted it creeping in at the Royal Festival Hall itself: 'The principal façade is towards the river, symmetrical, with . . . just one motif which betrays the new urge for something decorative – the curious stone apron in the middle of the top storey. There are no sufficient structural reasons for it; it was an afterthought, quite evidently, because the smooth dignified plainness of before was not considered enough.' And he goes on to wonder whether he is not already old-fashioned to doubt the validity of applied ornament to such a building.

To recognize the central position of spatial control in Pevsner's criticism of architecture also helps us to understand his attitude to earlier periods. The Perpendicular style – one achievement of the Middle Ages that was wholly peculiar to this country – however daring in its sacrifice of wall to window, however thrilling in its insistent repetitions, was not for him so impressive in its aspirations as the style which had preceded it, the Decorated. English buildings of the Decorated period, the first third of the fourteenth century, were a source of endless interest and delight. The men who designed the Octagon at Ely or the choir of Bristol Cathedral were as fascinated with the manipulation of space as Pevsner himself, and outstandingly ingenious in the effects they achieved. And at that period, in the medium not of iron and concrete but of fine quality freestone, an exquisite and natural vocabulary of mouldings and decorative sculpture was at hand to invigorate these structures and make them still more delectable.

The management of space in quite another context, the Picturesque of the eighteenth century, was another of Pevsner's preoccupations. Here he was able also to acknowledge the pioneer contribution of English thought and design. The relationship of buildings to landscape was a recurring theme on the pages of the *Architectural Review*, the earliest protagonist in this country of Modern architecture, on whose editorial board Pevsner sat for thirty years from the early 1940s. The effect on buildings even of lawns could rouse him, as for example at King's College, Cambridge, where the 'two big lawns E and W of Gibbs' Building are the most memorable piece of visual planning . . . exactly right in conjunction with the straightness and bigness of the chapel and Gibbs' Building.' Picturesque landscape provoked proportionately greater eloquence, as for instance the Rievaulx Terraces (*Yorkshire: North Riding*): 'The terrace itself is wide and gently curved. Groups of trees come forward and retire backward in an ever-changing rhythm. The bank towards the Rye is steep and wooded, and every so often views are cut open of the abbey deep down below and always at a different angle . . . The whole composition of the terrace is a superlative example of large-scale landscape gardening and of that unquestioning sense of being on top of the world which the rich and the noble in England possessed throughout the Georgian period.' His summary of Stourhead (*Wiltshire*), however, is the fullest exposition of his feelings on the subject: 'In thinking back of the whole of the grounds of Stourhead and especially the walk round the lake, the reader may agree with the writer that English picturesque landscaping of the C18 is the most beautiful form of gardening ever created . . . The aim was an ideal nature, acceptable as nature (and often even today accepted as nature by the layman), but contrived with superior skill and sensibility, and of course with a view entirely to later generations than one's own. This is perhaps the most astonishing thought produced by a day at Stourhead.'

England is *par excellence* the home of ruins, and Pevsner revelled in them, as he revelled in the eighteenth-century taste which had made so many of them into objects of picturesque attraction. But although they inspired some of his most eloquent flights, Pevsner the historian was also alive to their interest as archaeological documents. This led him to be lenient to scholarly reconstructions, regardless of any resulting picturesque loss. At Brinkburn Priory (*Northumberland*), for which 'No more enchanted spot could have been found', the reroofing of the church in 1858 was justified because 'architecturally, in the proper serious sense of the word, nothing has been lost'. Particularly revealing, and typically even-handed, are his comments on the over-restored church at Little Maplestead (*Essex*), remarkable for its circular nave: 'Those who believe in texture and the handiwork of the medieval mason will not be pleased by Little Maplestead . . . But those who are looking for design and composition can still enjoy the noble rotunda.'

Pevsner's appreciation of the Picturesque must have been an important factor in his predisposition to take the architecture of the nineteenth century seriously. Symmetry, one of the cardinal assumptions of design in the classical style, had given way in the years after 1800 to the serious exploitation of asymmetry, for Gothic first and subsequently for classical buildings too, and this introduced possibilities of surprise, which Pevsner always enjoyed, and also encouraged the bold massing of forms. For him the asymmetry of the Park front of Scott's Foreign Office was more admirable than the symmetry of its front to Whitehall, the asymmetrical handling of Street's Law Courts more deserving of respect than the nearly symmetrical façade of Waterhouse's Manchester Town Hall.

But in his assessment of the nineteenth-century architecture of England the classical and the Gothic did not stand equal. He accepted the cogency of Pugin's functional polemic on behalf of Gothic, seeing that it applied to more than just the style that Pugin himself championed to the exclusion of all others. But in the mid nineteenth century it was of course the Gothicists whom Pugin inspired. Pevsner's own appreciation of nobility, restraint and balance led him to award the highest marks among the Victorian Goths to J. L. Pearson, whose vaulted churches were always a source of pleasure for him, and to G. E. Street. The idiosyncratic Butterfield, in spite of his originality, Pevsner found it harder to admire, seeing in the insistent patterning so dear to this architect an example of the over-elaboration which for Pevsner marred almost all the products of the High Victorian age, swelling in the over-confidence of its burgeoning capitalism.

Perhaps Pevsner also felt that Gothic supremacy in England at this time was in part a reflection of its relatively greater success in this country in preceding centuries. The magniloquence of the Italian Renaissance and the spatial mastery of German or Austrian Baroque he hardly ever found equalled on this side of the Channel. Palladianism bored him, and the ever popular decorative style of Adam did not need his advocacy. But England did have its own version of Baroque in the architecture of Wren and his successors, Vanbrugh and Hawksmoor, to whose achievements Pevsner gave their full due. He also relished the neo-classicism of Soane and some of his 'primitivist' contemporaries, strongly influenced, as he saw, by Continental ideas – by the visions of Piranesi and the 'revolutionary' architecture of France.

Now for one final very important enthusiasm. William Morris was the first of Pevsner's 'pioneers', the progenitor of Arts and Crafts, which in its turn led on to the achievements of the German architects and designers who founded the Modern Movement in the early years of the twentieth century. Pevsner found Morris even more sympathetic as an artist and architectural propagandist than he did as an art theorist, where a tendency to look backward was, he admitted, a limitation. So Morris glass was always warmly commended, and the products of other great Victorian stained-glass firms such as Hardman or Clayton & Bell were judged by the standards of Morris. Similarly Pevsner heartily approved Morris's anti-scrape campaign against the drastic restoration which had deprived so many medieval churches of the evidence both of past human activity and of the action of time on materials. An unrestored church Pevsner always viewed with pleasure, perfectly summarized at Stragglethorpe (*Lincolnshire*): 'The church has a happily unchanged interior, crowded and alive.' When in its progress *The Buildings of England* reached Oxford in the early 1970s, after the great campaign of refacing the historic stone buildings was virtually completed, Pevsner noted those which had so far escaped: '[All Souls College front quadrangle] has not been face-lifted yet. It is a blessing.'

To Arts and Crafts architecture Pevsner awarded high praise. Much of it seemed to him not only forward-looking but also to embody almost everything that was best about English architectural traditions. Here was a style that seemed natural, deriving from the inherent qualities of building materials, a style that could in the hands of a Voysey be as serious, pure and astringent as a Perpendicular church, but a style that could also receive as ornament stylized foliage, flowers and trees, and could indulge in fancy and even whimsicality, just as his beloved Decorated had done six centuries before.

Pevsner's influence on the appreciation of architecture – as profound as his writings are voluminous – was transmitted as much through the spoken as through the printed word. He broadcast regularly, and he was a tireless lecturer, in the evenings at Birkbeck College, London, where he became professor of architectural history in 1959, weekly for a term each year at Cambridge, where his success as Slade Professor guaranteed him a packed audience year after year, and on frequent occasions elsewhere to audiences learned and lay. Always he endeavoured to explain and to persuade. When he first lectured on the Victorian designer Matthew Digby Wyatt, at a time when the period was little appreciated, he had to tell his audience to stop laughing because he was quite serious; on another occasion he made a memorable attempt to find an appropriate framework for judging Victorian architecture by dividing it into four categories: the good-good, the bad-good, the good-bad and the bad-bad.

As a Penguin author Pevsner fulfilled Allen Lane's ideal, combining authority with the passionate desire to communicate and to open new worlds to the reader. He enlarged the architectural appreciation of his adopted fellow-countrymen by making them aware of what they scarcely knew existed. The publication of each new volume of *The Buildings of England* transformed a county for its readers. The bulk of the fresh information concerned the nineteenth century, and by opening so many eyes to the virtues of Victorian architecture he has doubtless saved for future generations many a building which would otherwise have been demolished without a thought. It is not for nothing that Pevsner was chairman of the Victorian Society for so many years. Yet the correspondence he received from users of the series, which still continues to flow in, shows that it is his assessments of medieval buildings that have roused readers to the fullest expression of their own views. And that surely must have pleased him, for there is no doubt that for Pevsner himself it was in the Middle Ages that the awe, the thrill, and the joy of English architecture lay.

John Newman

The Best

Buildings of England

Anglo-Saxon:
seventh to eleventh centuries

For four centuries most Saxon churches remained modest, although the quality of the decorative art associated with them was often high. By the eleventh century buildings were beginning to reflect the more ambitious scale of Early Romanesque architecture on the Continent.

1] St John the Evangelist, Escomb, County Durham
Seventh century

Escomb is one of the very few surviving stone churches belonging to the earliest phase of Anglo-Saxon Christianity.

One of the most important and most moving survivals of the architecture of the times of Bede. It is Northumbrian in its tall, narrow proportions. Long nave and narrower chancel separated by a chancel arch which with its plain responds (differing from each other) is yet the only piece of decoration in the church. The masonry is excellent, of large blocks, probably of Roman origin, from Vinovium. The jambs of the chancel arch have carefully fitted long-and-short work. The same typically Anglo-Saxon technique at the angles of the building. The surviving windows are extremely small with deep splays inside, especially at the foot.
[COUNTY DURHAM]

26

2] St John the Baptist, Barnack, Cambridgeshire
Christ in Majesty, Late Saxon

This remarkable small sculpture may have formed part of an altarpiece. Its low-relief carving is in the Saxon tradition, but its monumental character associates it with continental early Romanesque art of the eleventh century.

Seated Christ in Majesty, relief, Late Saxon, and of exquisite quality. The draperies are managed as competently as never again anywhere for a century or more, and the expression is as human, dignified, and gentle as also never again anywhere for a century.
[BEDFORDSHIRE AND THE COUNTY OF HUNTINGDON AND PETERBOROUGH]

3] Holy Trinity, Great Paxton, Cambridgeshire
Crossing, eleventh century

Great Paxton provides rare evidence of the lines along which English architecture might have developed had the Norman Conquest not taken place.

There are very few Anglo-Saxon buildings one can call grandiose. Stow in Lincolnshire is one, Great Paxton is without doubt another. Yet on approaching the building, no-one can form any idea what is in store.

   The interior is not only a surprise, it is also an architectural shock of a high order. This was a cruciform church with a true crossing, and it was an aisled church. Both in pre-Conquest times are extreme rarities. The date of the church is not known, but it is not likely to be earlier than 1000. As for the crossing, a true crossing means that it is as wide as the nave, as the chancel, and as the transepts. This was a matter of course in Romanesque architecture on the Continent at that date, but it does not even apply to Stow. It does, however, apply to Great Paxton, as is fully displayed in the north transept arch. The responds are four big demi-shafts with thin shafts between. They carry lumpy, shapeless capitals and a plain abacus, and then the unmoulded arch is thrown across at a height unparalleled in early English architecture.

[BEDFORDSHIRE AND THE COUNTY OF HUNTINGDON AND PETERBOROUGH]

Norman Churches and Monasteries:
late eleventh to late twelfth centuries

The Norman Conquest coincided with the development of the mature Romanesque style. In England, as all over Europe, major churches and ample, well-organized domestic buildings were built to cater for the elaborate rituals and expanding communities of both new and reformed monasteries. By the twelfth century Romanesque architecture combined a sophisticated handling of elevations with increasing technical expertise in the mastery of stone vaulting. A lively repertoire of architectural ornament developed, whose cosmopolitan sources were reflected even in small parish churches and their furnishings.

4] St Mary, Lastingham, North Yorkshire
Crypt of the abbey church, rebuilt in the late eleventh century

The crude but robust detail reflects the influence of the architecture of Normandy in the first years after the Conquest.

A monastery formed at Lastingham by St Cedd in 654 and destroyed by the Danes in the later ninth century was re-founded in 1078 by Stephen of Whitby, first abbot of St Mary, York. Serious building must have been started at once and been pursued with great energy, for much, if by no means all, of the church was standing when at a date before 1086 the site was abandoned, and the monks moved to St Mary in York or, as this was only founded in 1088, its predecessor St Olave.

 The unforgettable crypt, of *c.* 1078–*c.* 1085, consists of a square part subdivided by four exceedingly short, thick columns into nine low compartments with groin-vaults. The columns have mighty capitals with coarse volutes and also primitive upright leaves or in their stead short intersecting arches, a very odd motif for a capital. Similar capitals to the responds of the short crypt chancel and the crypt apse.

[YORKSHIRE: THE NORTH RIDING]

5] Durham Cathedral
Interior of the nave, completed 1133

Durham is the supreme example of how Anglo-Norman architecture had developed its own character by the early twelfth century.

The impression of the nave is overpowering. The forms which surround the visitor are domineering to the utmost, without, however, being brutal. The force of the impact is conducted with a supreme mastery. The size of Durham is not greater than that of our other Norman cathedrals. The nave is 201 ft long by 39 ft wide and 73 ft high. That compares, for instance, with the 248 by 40 by 72 ft of Ely or the 174 by 34 by 68 ft of Gloucester. Yet the effect is quite different. That has chiefly two reasons: one the design and proportions of the elevations, the other the shape of the chief members used.

As for the elevation, it consists of nave arcade, gallery, and clerestory, as in nearly all major Norman churches of England and Normandy. But it could be interpreted in two ways in the direction from west to east and in two ways in the direction from floor to roof. Concerning the first, all piers could be identical or nearly so, as at Saint-Étienne in Caen and Ely, in which case a rapid and uninterrupted progress towards the altar is symbolized, or they could be of alternating shapes, every second pier being superordinate in design and every second subordinate. This was done in Normandy at Jumièges c. 1035–65, and it is done at Durham, whose compound piers alternate with circular ones. In this case progress towards the east is slower, every two bays being felt as one square major bay. One is inclined to halt in the middle of each of these major bays and take them in centrally. This experience can be had at Jumièges as at Durham, but whereas at Jumièges the subordinate columns are indeed subordinate, at Durham they are given an enormity of size which in the end remains the distinctive feature of the whole cathedral. These columns or round piers are 27 ft high and nearly 7 ft in diameter. The monument to James Britton in the nave, with the deceased reclining comfortably on a mattress on which he has placed an open book, could be put inside one of the piers, and if he had a moderator lamp he could continue reading and musing in that circular cell. Moreover, the piers are patterned in nobly scaled grooved designs. So everything is done to give them the utmost importance, and it is the mighty impact of the piers from left and right which makes one feel so utterly overwhelmed. But there is nothing savage in this attack. The proportions are actually handled with a sense of balance rarely achieved in the Norman style. One has to study the elevation to appreciate that.

At Durham the gallery is neither too large nor too small. It is there in its own right, yet can never compete with the cyclopic arcade. The actual proportion of gallery to arcade is 5:2. Niceness of proportions is so rarely aimed at in early medieval buildings on such a large scale that, if one has not been to Durham for a long time and has only seen the cathedral in the meantime in occasional postcards or illustrations, one is every time shocked by the sheer bigness of everything, starting from the blank arcading along the outer walls of the aisles which is no more than an enrichment of the dado of the walls and yet has columns of more than the height of a man.

[COUNTY DURHAM]

34

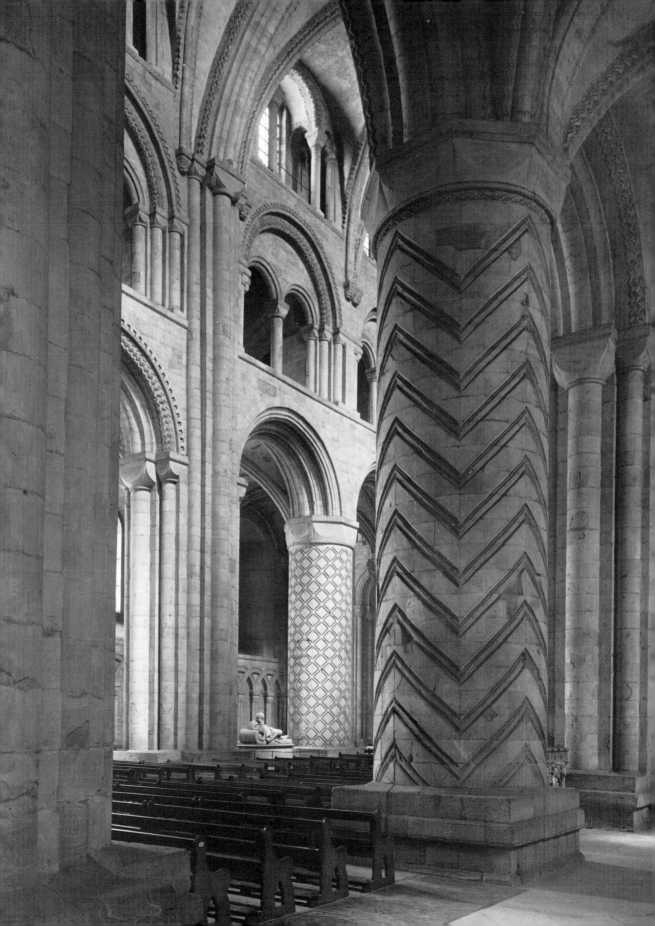

6] St Mary and St David, Kilpeck, Hereford and Worcester
c. 1134–40

By this time stone parish churches were widespread, but Kilpeck is exceptional in its wealth of ornament, the work of a group of sculptors active in the western counties.

One of the most perfect Norman village churches in England, small but extremely generously decorated, and also uncommonly well preserved. The red sandstone must have been selected with great acumen to have stood up so well to eight hundred years of wear and tear, and Cottingham's restoration of 1848 seems to have been a competent and disciplined job. A comparison between G. R. Lewis's lithographs of 1842 and the building as it is now shows that not much has been lost over the last four or five generations. If the church is so sumptuous, the reason was the presence of a Benedictine priory, founded in 1134 as a cell of Gloucester, and of the castle. The church may well have been begun immediately after 1134. The sculpture of its south doorway is so close to Shobdon, which must be of *c.* 1140–5, that the date makes sense.

The church is designed on the simple plan of nave, chancel, apse, in decreasing width and height. The exterior is articulated by means of flat buttresses and clasping corner buttresses. A corbel table runs all round, decorated with flat zigzag, rope, etc., and the corbels are the best preparation for the profusion of decorative sculpture and fantasy throughout the church. Of motifs there are the Lamb and Cross, a dog and a rabbit, two wrestlers, a sheila-na-gig (all these apse), another Lamb and Cross (chancel), and many heads. The corbels are clearly not all by the same hand – the best have an irresistible comic-strip character – and not by the hand of the brilliant master of the south doorway.

The south doorway is sumptuously decorated but not sumptuous. One order of decorated shafts and decorated jambs, decorated voussoirs in two orders, tympanum. In the tympanum simply a Tree of Life, beaded and with thick grapes. Vertical zigzag on the lintel. The outer order of the arch has linked medallions inhabited by dragons, birds, etc. In the inner order are beakheads – a motif which reached Herefordshire probably by way of Leominster, as it is a Reading motif – and also heads and a flying angel, all radially arranged. The shafts are decorated very much like those of Shobdon, one with symmetrical trails and palmettes, the other with two splendid long wiry figures, one on top of the other, and both enmeshed in wild, thin trails. The tight clothes with close parallel folds like ribs are unmistakable. On the jambs hideous fat and long dragons, one snaking up, the other down, and in the abaci a head with beaded trails coming out of the mouth, and a pair of affronted dragons. The sources of this sculpture are varied. The fat snake-like dragons are purely Viking, of the so-called Ringerike style. The figures on one shaft are very different, nimble, lively, and ready to jump. For them no source has yet been found; for although the founder of Shobdon Priory had visited Santiago de Compostela and although on the Puerta de las Platerias figures also stand on top of each other, the style is entirely different.

[HEREFORDSHIRE]

36

7] Bristol Cathedral, Avon
Late Norman chapter house, built *c.* 1150–70 for the Augustinian abbey
founded in 1140

*The size and grandeur of this chapter house, used for the daily meetings of the monastic
community, are typical of major abbeys such as this Augustinian house founded in 1140.*

The chapter house is completely Late Norman, i.e. of *c.* 1150–70. It is rib-vaulted, in two high
and large bays. The transverse arches are flat with rolls left and right. The flat top has two
zigzags affronted, as it were, to form a frieze of lozenges. The cross ribs have bold zigzags. The
decoration of the north and south walls is a striking example of what animated effects the Late
Norman style can achieve with nothing but abstract material. Lowest tier with the same blank
arches or shallow niches as in the vestibule. Upper tier with a blank arcade of intersected arches,
the shafts alternatingly plain and spiral-fluted with beading, the arches all spiral-fluted with
beading and a little nailhead. Then the large lunettes, patterned in such a way that again the
effect is that of enriched zigzag work. Yet only one of the four lunettes has an actual un-
intermittent band of vertical zigzag. The others are rather like diagonally interwoven strands.
The west wall is different (with a lunette filled by arcading with intersected arches which rise
absurdly to the apex and then fall again).
[NORTH SOMERSET AND BRISTOL]

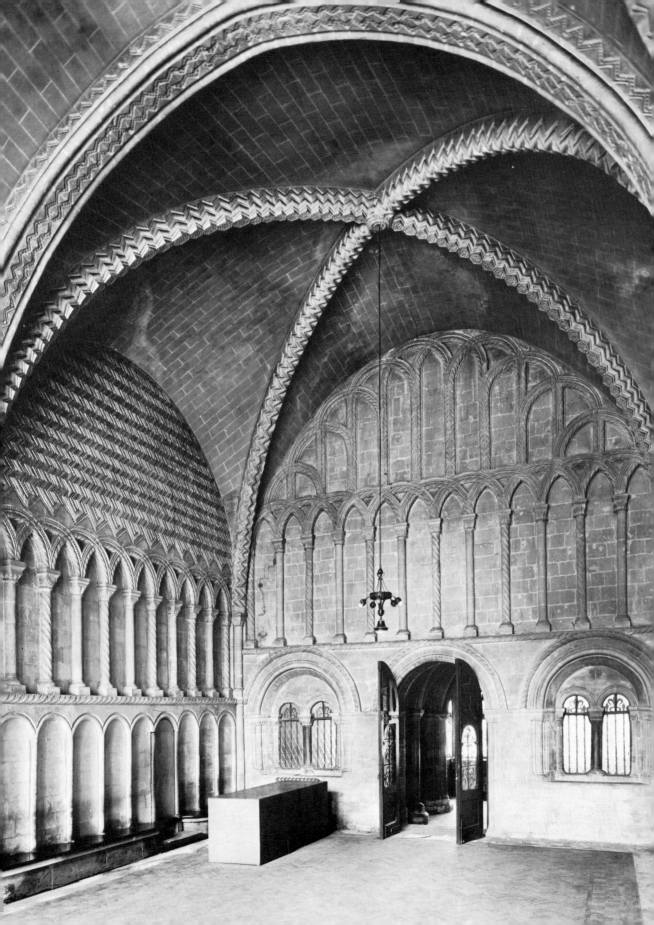

8] Malmesbury Abbey, Wiltshire
Late Norman sculpture in the south porch of the former
Benedictine abbey (now St Mary's church),
founded in the seventh century, rebuilt in the twelfth

*Malmesbury is one of the rare cases of a major English Romanesque church whose entrance is
lavishly decorated with figure sculpture in the French manner.*

The south porch is the *chef d'œuvre* of Malmesbury, among the best pieces of Norman sculpture
and decoration in England. Inside the porch, above some uninspired blank arcading, are two
lunettes facing each other, each with six seated apostles and an angel flying horizontally above
their heads. The figures are very elongated (like those in medallions on the outer arch of the
porch, which seem to be inspired by the west of France), but whereas the use of the side walls of a
porch for scenes is south-west French (Moissac, Souillac), the style of the figures here depends on
that of Burgundy about 1130, and the quality approaches that of Autun. In England the nearest
parallel is one panel on the west front of Lincoln Cathedral, about twenty years earlier than
Malmesbury.

[WILTSHIRE]

9] Fountains Abbey, North Yorkshire
Ruins of the monastery begun in 1135 and rebuilt
in the later twelfth and early thirteenth centuries

The Cistercian order was established in Burgundy in the early twelfth century in reaction against
the luxury and elaborate ritual of older Benedictine monasteries. Its rules prescribed plain,
unadorned buildings; later on attitudes became more lax, as the early-sixteenth-century tower at
Fountains demonstrates.

There is no other place in the country in which the mind can so readily evoke the picture of
thirteenth-century monastic life, and the eye a picture of the vast extent and yet the crispness and
freshness of Cistercian architecture in the wild North Country forests. Fountains is the pattern in
England and even beyond England of the arrangement of the monastic quarters of a large
Cistercian house. The buildings are planned along the river Skell, which gives water for the
brewing, washing, and drainage. The layout of the range round the cloister accords with the
universal Cistercian standard and differs only in details from the general Benedictine traditions.

The approach to the inner bailey, that is the west range of the cloister, must have been
overwhelmingly impressive in the twelfth and thirteenth centuries and is still one of the most
impressive experiences of monastic architecture in England. This long, even wall with well-
spaced windows represented a world of exacting order unmatched in the secular world. The west
range had cellars in its north parts, the refectory of the lay-brethren in its larger south part. The
north part is Late Norman; on the ground floor small round-headed double-chamfered windows
and four double-chamfered doorways. The whole upper floor was the dormitory of the lay-
brethren.

[YORKSHIRE: THE WEST RIDING]

Norman Military Architecture

The Normans introduced the stone castle to England. The unsettled state of the country and the rivalry between aristocratic factions ensured that castles continued to be constructed throughout the twelfth century.

10] Castle Rising, Norfolk
Keep, mid twelfth century

Castle Rising illustrates the best known type, a defensive enclosure within which the keep was the most important building.

The castle was built by William de Albini about the middle of the twelfth century. He married the widowed queen of Henry I, was made Earl of Sussex, and died in 1176. The principal surviving part is the keep, but there were plenty of other buildings, and there still are very mighty earthworks, covering an area of 12 acres. The main enclosure is roughly circular, and has a circumference of 1000 yards. The main ditch goes down to a depth of nearly 60 ft, and the rampart is about 64 ft high.

The keep is one of the largest and one of the most decorated in England. It is a companion piece to the yet grander Norwich keep. Both are of the type known as hall keeps as against the more usual tower keeps, that is they are broader than they are high. The measurements at Castle Rising are $78\frac{1}{2}$ by $68\frac{1}{2}$ ft by a height of only about 50 ft. There were only a ground floor, inaccessible from outside, and a principal floor, although the latter was in parts again horizontally subdivided. The walls are over 8 ft thick and strengthened by shallow buttresses. Some of these are given the decorative enrichment of nook-shafts. The principal enrichment however is lavished on the east wall, or rather the staircase and forebuilding which are set in front of it. The staircase is entered from the south. Its south and much longer east wall have small decorative blank arcading, partly with intersected arches. To the south also medallions with heads of monsters. Castle Rising was no doubt built in imitation of Norwich although it is by no means as thorough in the application of blank arcading, the one decorative motif on which they both relied and on which Norman masons were so often satisfied to rely exclusively. The most remarkable thing is the fact that a military, that is entirely utilitarian, building was decorated externally at all.

The forebuilding has been called the best preserved in England. It has large windows on the floor where the staircase arrives. An upper storey was added in the fourteenth century.

[NORTH WEST AND SOUTH NORFOLK]

11] Orford Castle, Suffolk
Keep, 1165–73

Orford demonstrates a transitional type of castle design, soon to be outmoded by the growing importance of the curtain wall with mural towers.

 The keep was built for Henry II in 1165–73. It was a revolutionary design; for it seems the first in England to abandon the square or oblong shape in favour of a militarily more advantageous one. At Orford it is an irregular eighteen-sided shape to which was added a square staircase turret and two other square buttresses or turrets, although these really invalidated some of what had been gained by the polygonal centre. The angles of a polygon are less easily mined than the rectangles at the corners of a square keep and they are also more easily defended. Chilham in Kent and Odiham in Hampshire are the only other polygonal Norman keeps in England. But Henry II also built or remodelled the polygonal keep of Gisors in Normandy. Conisbrough in South Yorkshire, being circular, was an even better solution. This dates from *c*. 1180. By then more radical changes began to appear in defence technique which made even Conisbrough and Orford old-fashioned. Grey ashlar and septaria. Battered ashlar base. Forebuilding to which originally led an outer staircase. The doorway is placed askew. The chapel is in the forebuilding, the circular hall on the second and third floors.
[SUFFOLK]

46

Early English Gothic:
late twelfth to late thirteenth centuries

The principles of the Gothic style, which evolved in France during the twelfth century, were only gradually absorbed in England. But by the early thirteenth century the new style, with its light and spacious interiors unified by stone vaults with pointed arches, was beginning to develop its own particularly English features, for example the 'stiff-leaf' foliage carving that is such a hallmark of the period. This 'Early English' phase (as it was called by nineteenth-century antiquarians) was revolutionized from the mid thirteenth century by the influence of Westminster Abbey, newly rebuilt by Henry III, with large traceried windows in the latest French style.

12] Tynemouth Priory, Tyne and Wear
East end, *c.* 1190

The east extension of this Benedictine priory, dramatically sited on a rocky promontory above the mouth of the Tyne, illustrates the grandeur that could be achieved with simple early Gothic forms.

Enough stands of the Early English additions, begun *c.* 1190, to allow for a very strong aesthetic impact. The east wall of the rebuilt chancel belongs to the best Early English compositions we possess and has the additional advantage of a superb position, whether one sees the blue sky made a deeper blue by the frame of the lancet windows, or whether gusts of wind drive the rain through the unglazed openings. From outside the east wall is very sheer. No decoration at the foot, a group of three very tall stepped lancets with the plainest chamfered jambs and arches, separated and flanked by buttresses, a second row of windows, small lancets left and right and a vesica-shaped window in the middle, and then above this one more lancet. This alone has the decorative enrichment of stepped blank arcading left and right. It was inside the gable the lines of which are at once evident. In the fourteenth or fifteenth century, however, above all this another upper chamber or hall was built on top of the chancel and its vault, presumably for reasons of defence. It must have ruined thoroughly the calculated proportions of the Early English elevation.

[NORTHUMBERLAND]

13] St Mary, Church of the Knights Templar, The Temple, London
Choir, rebuilt *c.* 1220–40

*The enlargement of choirs to provide space for extra altars and more elaborate liturgical
ceremonies was frequent from the later twelfth century onwards.*

About 1220 a new enlarged chancel was begun. It was consecrated in 1240. It was, on the pattern
of the Winchester retrochoir and exactly contemporary with the Salisbury retrochoir, designed
on the hall principle, that is with aisles of the same height as the nave. In its proportions however
it has none of the excessive slimness of Winchester and Salisbury. It is in fact one of the most
perfectly and classically proportioned buildings of the thirteenth century in England, airy, yet
sturdy, generous in all its spacing, but disciplined and sharply pulled together. The measurements
are: height to vault 36 ft 3 in., to pier capitals 20 ft $10\frac{1}{2}$ in., that is roughly 3:2. Tall Purbeck piers
of the classic French Gothic section (cf. Salisbury, begun 1220): circular core with attached shafts
in the main axes. Moulded capitals. Quadripartite rib-vaults with elegantly moulded ribs. The
transverse arches are as thin as the ribs. Tall lancet windows in stepped groups of three. To the
interior they are shafted with detached Purbeck shafts. Only the east windows have in addition
head-stops, flat dish-like bosses of stiff-leaf foliage, and, in the centre group, two blank elongated
quatrefoils above the lower windows. Stiff-leaf bosses in the vault of the chancel 'nave'.
[LONDON I: THE CITIES OF LONDON AND WESTMINSTER]

14] Wells Cathedral, Somerset
Detail of the north porch, early thirteenth century

The lively decoration of wall surfaces was a recurrent preoccupation of English medieval architecture; rarely was it achieved with such subtlety and finesse as in this early Gothic porch at Wells.

The north porch is treated so sumptuously that we cannot be in any doubt where the principal entrance to the cathedral was meant to be. The inside of the porch is a masterpiece of the Early English style, of a richness which is at the same time orderly and measured. Two rib-vaulted bays; on detached double shafts in the corners, on triple shafts in the middles. The shafts have shaft-rings and stiff-leaf capitals. The walls are covered with tiers of arcading, first a tier of four blank pointed arches per bay with continuous moulding and spandrels filled with symmetrical stiff-leaf arrangements, then the sill-moulding with hanging sprays of stiff-leaf. The moulding is cut off at the ends of each bay by tailed monsters biting into it.

    The upper blank arcades are almost in two layers in so far as they have their own supporting shafts close to the wall but are separated from one another by two detached shafts standing behind one another. So there is much depth in this blank arcade, but depth in front of a clearly maintained back surface. That is Early English at its best and most English, in the same spirit as contemporary work at Lincoln, the cathedral which was built by St Hugh of Avallon, bishop of Lincoln. The shafts of this arcade again all have shaft-rings and stiff-leaf capitals. Arch mouldings with keels and fillets. The outer moulding of each arch intersects a little with that of the next immediately above the capitals. In the spandrels rings of stiff-leaf and also figure motifs.

[NORTH SOMERSET AND BRISTOL]

15] St Mary, West Walton, Norfolk
c. 1240

West Walton is one of the most splendid of the many large, aisled parish churches built in the thirteenth century in the newly drained fenlands of Norfolk and Lincolnshire. The free-standing tower is a local speciality, perhaps explained by unstable ground.

One of the most sumptuous Early English parish churches – not only of Norfolk. The date of nearly everything that remains is *c.* 1240; the source of the style is Lincoln – the parish churches more than the cathedral. The building is stone-faced. The tower stands completely detached at a distance to the south. It is pierced on the ground floor on all four sides. The angles are strengthened by big polygonal buttresses.

The interior of the church is distinguished by its arcades on circular piers with the detached Purbeck shafts (now in many cases humbly renewed in wood) and gorgeous stiff-leaf capitals. The nave has six bays and there were in addition two-bay chancel chapels. The piers had eight shafts in the chancel and have four shafts in the nave, and all have shaft-rings. The arches have many mouldings. In the chapels they have hoodmoulds on big leaf paterae. The clerestory is original too. The windows are of a single light, set outside under small arches so that only every third contains a window, but inside in larger blank arcading so that every other arch contains a window. This is a specially happy conceit. The chancel arch goes with the arcades, but is of course taller, which leads to some awkward junctions.

[NORTH WEST AND SOUTH NORFOLK]

16] Salisbury Cathedral, Wiltshire
Tomb of Bishop Giles de Bridport, died 1262

Early tombs with effigies were low and uncovered; the provision of a carved canopy in the manner of a shrine is an innovation of the thirteenth century. Purbeck marble from Dorset was especially popular for such monuments.

The tomb stands between chancel aisle and east aisle of the south-east transept, a marvellous monument of Purbeck and stone. Purbeck effigy, beardless, under a pointed cinquefoiled head canopy. Turrets to its left and right. Two angels also left and right. The bishop raises both hands. The effigy lies in a shrine-like architecture open in two twin openings to north and south. To the north they are of Purbeck marble, to the south of stone. They consist each of pointed-trefoiled arches and a quatrefoiled circle over. All this is pierced work, i.e. bar tracery, and the earliest occurrence at Salisbury of this important motif, some five or ten years before the cloisters, though over fifteen years after Westminster Abbey. Stiff-leaf sprays. The upper parts are of stone on both sides. Gables on dragons, small heads between the arches and the gables. The gables again with leaf sprays, just on the point of abandoning the stiff-leaf convention. Scenes from the life of the bishop in the spandrels, again earlier than in the chapter house. The scenes are unrestored. Slender figures and much relished landscape elements. Shrine-like roof as a top. On it stiff-leaf crockets and finials.
[WILTSHIRE]

17] Hereford Cathedral
North transept, *c.* 1260, and tomb of Bishop Aquablanca, died 1268

Both architecture and tomb display the preoccupation with the new tracery forms introduced in the mid thirteenth century at Westminster Abbey.

With the north transept we are on the highest level of architectural art. It was no doubt planned by Bishop Aquablanca, who died in 1268 and is buried in it, and the motifs so evidently derived from Westminster Abbey make a start before *c.* 1250 or 1255 all but impossible. The east arcade is of two bays with astringent, almost straight-sided arches. Compound piers with stone shafts and also Purbeck shafts – again an import from Westminster Abbey. The Purbeck shafts have shaft-rings. Thick, rich stiff-leaf capital on the pier (which the Abbey has not), moulded capitals on the responds. Handsome little stiff-leaf sprigs on the bases. One big entirely under-cut dogtooth moulding in the arch. Hoodmoulds on head-stops. Vaulting-shafts on deliberately thin corbels. Blank gallery of two triple openings to each bay below. Thinly cusped, again almost straight-sided arches – all structural elements in this transept are thin. Three encircled quatrefoils in bar tracery above. The arches of course again nearly straight-sided. The diapering above, direct from Westminster Abbey, has been re-cut in the nineteenth century. The famous Westminster clerestory windows of spherical-triangle form have very deep, stepped sills to the inside.

Bishop Aquablanca's tomb stands between the chancel aisle and the transept which he created. The architecture is more important now than the sculpture; for the effigy is defaced, and cannot compete with the spare, incisive architecture of the canopy with its steeply erect gables.
[HEREFORDSHIRE]

18] St Cosmas and St Damian, Boyton, Wiltshire
South chapel, *c.* 1280

Chapels attached to parish churches to commemorate families or individuals were not uncommon, but few have the panache of Boyton.

The south chapel makes it certain that no architectural traveller will forget Boyton. The west window is a tour-de-force, a little showy perhaps but certainly powerful. It is an exaggeratedly large circular window with three quatrefoiled spherical triangles and between them three circles each filled by three small circles. Bar tracery appears at Salisbury Cathedral only about 1270, and the tracery here is a little in advance of Salisbury. One might date the chapel *c.* 1280, and that date agrees with the fact that Walter Giffard, Archbishop of York, obtained the church before he died in 1279, and that his brother, Godfrey, Bishop of York, in 1279 made elaborate liturgical provisions for the chapel. It was probably founded to commemorate their brother Sir Alexander.
[WILTSHIRE]

Decorated Gothic:
late thirteenth to mid fourteenth centuries

In this period of confident originality, bold and unexpected spatial effects were combined with a wealth of innovative patterns in both vaults and window tracery. Delicate sculpture was lavished on major buildings as well as on the monuments and furnishings of smaller churches.

19] Eleanor Cross, Geddington, Northamptonshire
c. 1295

The peripatetic nature of the royal court was one means by which new styles were widely disseminated.

Queen Eleanor had died at Harby in Nottinghamshire in November 1290. Edward I decided to set up crosses on lavishly decorated substructures at the places where the funeral cortège had halted overnight. The same had been done in France for the body of King Louis IX in 1271. The stopping places were Lincoln, Grantham, Stamford, Geddington, Hardingstone, Stony Stratford, Dunstable, St Albans, Waltham, Cheapside, and finally Charing Cross. Most of the places chosen had royal castles or monastic houses of distinction. Of all these crosses only the three of Hardingstone and Geddington in Northamptonshire and Waltham in Hertfordshire survive.

The cross at Geddington, erected shortly after 1294, is the most modest and the best preserved. Its shape heralds the end of the classic Gothic moment and the coming of Decorated capriciousness. Triangular and carrying on at the top, by means of six pinnacles, to a recessed hexagonal star with more pinnacles. Close diapering in the lower parts. The three figures in the three niches characteristic also of the end of the crisp and sharp carving of up to 1275–80 and the heavier flow and broader masses of 1290 etc.
[NORTHAMPTONSHIRE]

20] Wells Cathedral, Somerset
Retrochoir, early fourteenth century

This low rectangular area between high altar and Lady Chapel (the prosaic English counterpart to the curved French ambulatory) was transformed by the early-fourteenth-century master of Wells into a space of great complexity.

The retrochoir with its chapels is part of the same ingenious spatial conceit as the Lady Chapel to its east. All looks square and rectangular and normal from outside – like Salisbury e.g. But inside the sensitive visitor is at once thrown into a pleasing confusion. There are six clustered shafts in the retrochoir plus the two intermediate piers at the east end of the chancel itself. It takes time to realize why they are placed as they are. The two easternmost shafts are part of the Lady Chapel octagon. Then there are piers to mark the west ends of the two eastern side chapels, the chapels which flank the Lady Chapel. They naturally stand in axis with the chapel walls. Moreover they are in axis with the arcade between chancel and chancel aisles, and they form part of the initial rectangularity. But the next two clusters a little to the west of these are again in axis with the Lady Chapel west piers. That is unexpected, in fact unnecessary, but it is where the designer reveals his genius. For by this means, floating in the open space of the retrochoir, an elongated hexagon is formed – at right angles to the elongated octagon of the Lady Chapel. That the two intermediate piers of the east arcade of the chancel are not placed so as to be in line with the west piers of the hexagon is an additional complication which, instead of heightening the aesthetic significance of the whole, only involved the designer in unnecessary difficulties as soon as he had to invent and set out vaults. It will be realized that in several places odd triangular spaces would have to be vaulted, and the master makes his appreciation of this known by giving the west pier of either east chapel a triangular shape. The Decorated style always liked the diagonal and so also the triangle. Yet however one sorts it out, there was bound to remain *Resträume*, as Dehio called them when he wrote his classic analysis of Vierzehnheiligen.

It will no doubt by now be obvious to anyone who has tried to follow this description that English Decorated space can be as intricate and as thrilling as German Rococo space. The vaults here are all of the new lierne kind except for the east chapels which are easily disposed of by diagonal ribs, ridge-ribs, and one set of tiercerons. The transepts, being square, could again receive a lierne star without much difficulty, though one should remember that liernes were still a very new toy. But the centre was the problem, and the combination here of lierne stars of various patterns with the triangles. How it is done cannot be described and only be drawn by the expert. But one should not shirk the effort of understanding it. It is like penetrating a piece of complicated polyphonic music.

[NORTH SOMERSET AND BRISTOL]

64

21] Bristol Cathedral, Avon
Choir aisle of the former Augustinian abbey, early fourteenth century

The rebuilding of the eastern arm of the abbey church, to a design unique in English Gothic, was begun by Abbot Knowle in 1298.

The choir with its aisles is the great surprise of Bristol. For Bristol is a hall-church, that is a church in which the aisles are of the same height as the nave, a type of design which was to become the *leitmotif* of late Gothic architecture in Germany, but appears here, perhaps for the first time in Europe, with its spatial potentialities fully realized.

The weight of the choir vault is conveyed to the outer aisle walls by a device which more than anything makes the Bristol interior unforgettable. There are, one might say, flying buttresses thrown across the aisles at the level of the springing of the vaults, but they are given the form of bridges from arcade pier to outer wall. Each bridge can be compared with – and might indeed be inspired by – a tie-beam on arched braces in a timber roof. Big mouchette-shaped openings in the spandrels, big enough to look through them into neighbouring aisle vaults with ease. The aisle vaults again are something of consummate ingenuity. They can essentially be defined as transverse tunnel-vaults, an effective method of buttressing (see e.g. Fountains Abbey in England). But they consist here of two bays of rib-vaulting with longitudinal (that is transverse) ridge-ribs. The flash of genius in the arrangement is that in each little vault the cell resting on the bridge is simply left out. That makes the transverse arch and ribs on the middle of the bridge stand as it were on tiptoes, a tightrope feat right up there. It also allows us to look yet more freely from vault to vault. The hall-elevation as such makes for diagonal vistas across a whole room at eye-level, to an extent impossible and indeed undesirable to the thirteenth century. Now this hankering after spatial surprise is extended to the vaulting zone, that is vistas are opened up not only diagonally across but also diagonally up.
[NORTH SOMERSET AND BRISTOL]

66

22] Ely Cathedral, Cambridgeshire
Octagon, after 1322

After the Norman crossing tower collapsed in 1322, rebuilding took the ambitious form of an octagon covering a much enlarged area, an unprecedented solution, made possible by the vital contribution of William Hurley, one of the most original carpenters of his age.

The Octagon is a delight from beginning to end for anyone who feels for space as strongly as for construction. For the basic emotion created by the Octagon as one approaches it along the nave is one of spaciousness, a relief, a deep breath after the oppressive narrowness of the Norman work. Then follows, as one tries to account for that sudden widening of one's lungs, the next moment's feeling, a feeling of surprise. Its immediate cause is that light falls in from large windows diagonally – a deviation unheard of in the church architecture of the West. The rhythm of the Octagon as one takes it in, once one has reached its centre, is an alternation of immensely tall arches in the main directions and of a three-tier arrangement in the diagonals, consisting of arches of arcade height, a kind of blind triforium above, and the large 'clerestory' windows. The arches, the tall ones too, have capitals only to some of their jamb mouldings. Hoodmoulds rest on excellently carved head-stops. The blind triforium consists in each diagonal of three ogee niches of odd trefoil shape, filled by seated Victorian figures. The windows have rather gross and heavy flowing tracery.

The vault is of wood, of the tierceron kind, and shoots up with its palm branches from each of the eight angles to one side of the eight-sided lantern balancing on the vault. It seems a miraculous feat, though in fact the lantern is of timber and hence not as heavy as it seems, and though it does not really stand on the vaulting-ribs, but on a magnificent sturdy timber construction behind the vaults.

The lantern, as will be noticed with delight, does not stand angle above angle and side above side with the masonry octagon, but with a twist, so that each outer side faces an inner angle, and vice versa. It seems the *nec plus ultra* of that playing with spatial surprise which characterizes the Octagon altogether. But it has at the same time a sound functional reason. By means of that twist each of the reinforced angles of the masonry octagon shoots out diagonally two horizontal and two diagonally rising beams, and thereby the weight from each angle of the timber lantern is split at its foot and carried on diagonally by two pairs of principal beams. The whole, seen in a diagram, is much like a twentieth-century space frame. Standing inside, at the foot of the Octagon, however, one realizes nothing of all that and is simply thrilled and bewildered by the way in which eleven ribs sprout out of each angle shaft and five of them carry one side of the lantern. The lantern has large windows and is gloriously light.

[CAMBRIDGESHIRE]

23] Salisbury Cathedral, Wiltshire
Spire, begun in 1334

The seemingly effortless soaring spire was developed to perfection in the fourteenth century; another aspect of the Decorated preoccupation with the geometry of polygons.

The Early English cathedral was meant to have only a relatively low lantern tower. On top probably was a lead pyramid spire. The thirteenth-century stage of the tower, the one against which the roofs abut, has tall blank Early English arches with depressed trefoil heads. Shafts and stiff-leaf capitals. Then the Decorated work begins. Ballflower frieze and blank battlements and then two tall stages. They are studded everywhere with ballflower. Tall two-light windows with circles over. In these, on the lower stage, undulating foiling, on the upper subcusped foiling. All these motifs are an intelligent, up-to-date restating of Early English motifs of the cathedral. The angle buttresses start flat and set-back, but in the Decorated work turn polygonal, with the same kind of fine blank arches, tracery, and gables that we have found in the pinnacles of the flying buttresses added at the same time to help carry the tower and spire.

The spire is wonderfully slender, and the solution of the problem of how to reach the octagon from the square is perfect. Short crocketed pinnacles on the buttresses, in the middles of the sides at the foot of the spire lucarnes under crocketed gables and with pinnacles, and again at the corners taller inner pinnacles rising higher than the lucarnes. They are square, with their own angle buttresses and angle pinnacles, as it were. From a distance the effect varies. If you are inside the precinct the pinnacles keep close to the spire and the outline is almost like that of a broach-spire, except for just the slightest barbs. If you are in the meadows to the south or west the pinnacles speak individually and form a subordinate preamble to the spectacular rise of the spire.
[WILTSHIRE]

24] Butley Priory, Suffolk
Gatehouse, *c.* 1320–5

The use of local flint and stone to create surface patterns, as in this early example, became a special feature of the late medieval architecture of East Anglia.

The gatehouse is a most ambitious and interesting building of the fourteenth century. Its historical importance lies in the fact that the heraldry which is so lavishly displayed on it proves a date about 1320–5 and that it is thus the earliest datable building with flushwork decoration. Nor is the decoration used in any way hesitatingly. On the contrary, stimulated by the general trend of these years, which was all for the greatest luxuriance and elaboration (cf. e.g. Ely Lady Chapel), the designer of the Butley gatehouse got at once as much decorative vivacity out of it as any of his successors ever after. To the outside the gateway is divided into a pedestrian entrance with a finely and continuously moulded two-centred arch and a carriage entrance with an almost straight-sided depressed arch dying into the imposts, and then to the left and right two projecting bays no doubt meant to carry towers.

What demands the closest study is the decoration. On the north front there is flushwork with a cinquefoil and big mouchettes above the pedestrian entrance and pointed trefoils in the spandrels of the carriage entrance. On the buttresses to the left and right are niches. The north fronts of the projecting bays or tower-bases have each a large sham two-light window with flowing tracery in two different patterns. This is the most attractive decorative motif at Butley and occurs in several other places as well. The sham windows reach up as high as the niches in the buttresses, and higher than the entrance arches. Above these follows a large panel with thirty-five shields in five rows. Such a heraldic display on the gatehouse of a monastery had already been done in the late thirteenth century at Kirkham in Yorkshire.

Above the sham windows are straight-headed three-light windows with ogee-headed lights to the south. On the inner sides, i.e. towards the archway, the upper windows have shouldered lights, and below them is a gay chequerboard of flushwork on the left, the same motif in diapers on the right. In the middle, above the heraldry panel, there is one tall two-light window with renewed tracery and two sham windows of the same type to its left and right. These have flowing tracery with a wheel of five mouchettes. In the gable is a fine group of three niches, the left and right ones with straight-sided climbing arches, the middle one with a beautiful projecting canopy. All arches are cusped and subcusped.

[SUFFOLK]

72

25] Norwich Cathedral, Norfolk
Doorway to the church from the north walk of the cloister, *c.* 1310

The well preserved Norwich doorway is a reminder that most medieval sculpture, as here, was once enhanced by paint.

One of the most beautiful portals of the budding Decorated style, erected probably about the year 1310. Four detached shafts, and in the arch figures under crocketed ogee gables arranged radially: Christ seated in the middle, between angels, and then four more figures. Against the east wall three deep niches with crocketed ogee gables on head corbels. In the vault Christ in Limbo, a praying bishop and a praying monk, and foliage still naturalistic. There are also very fine bosses immediately against the wall, notably the four Evangelists. They are all perfect examples on a small scale of the style of sculpture in the early fourteenth century.
[NORTH EAST NORFOLK AND NORWICH]

74

26] St Bartholomew, Much Marcle, Hereford and Worcester
Tomb of Blanche Mortimer, Lady Grandison, died 1347

Sculpture of the Decorated period could combine idealized beauty with a realism not found in the remoter characterizations of the thirteenth century.

The effigy of Blanche Mortimer, Lady Grandison, is outstandingly beautiful and interesting. In a recess. The recess contains the tomb-chest, against which is cusped arcading with shields. The back wall has arcading too, and at the top coving with rather bare ribbing crossing at right angles. Then a canopy cants forward. It has pendant arches and panels with shields over. The wavy cresting with putto heads is clearly not original. But now the effigy. The head is strikingly beautiful and realistic, eyes closed, lips slightly parted. Beautiful hands with long fingers. The monument provides, moreover, the most surprising demonstration of realism, i.e. the will to deceive – for all this was of course originally painted – in the way the train of the long skirt hangs down over the tomb-chest. Here is an English counterpart to the illusionism which occurs at the same time in Italian painting and German sculpture.

[HEREFORDSHIRE]

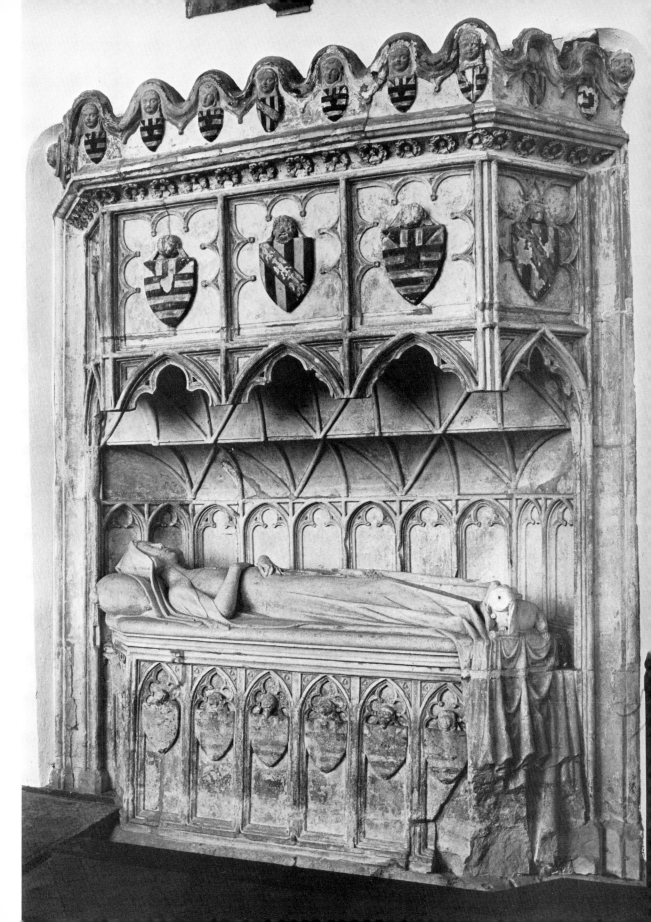

Perpendicular Gothic:
mid fourteenth to early sixteenth centuries

Walls became skeletal structures for large windows filled with rigorously rectilinear 'Perpendicular' tracery; stone fan-vaults or elaborate timberwork provided opportunities for virtuoso display by mason and carpenter. Towers of the great parish churches became the symbols of civic pride, their designs reflecting different regional traditions.

27] St Botolph, Boston, Lincolnshire
Tower, early fourteenth/early sixteenth century

Boston Stump is a tower of exceptional ambition, the product of three separate building phases.

Boston in the Middle Ages was a port of considerable importance, and St Botolph is a giant among English parish churches. The Stump, the most prodigious of English parochial steeples, is 272 ft high. It was apparently begun in 1309. The chancel asserts itself towards the market place, the steeple with unforgettable force towards the river, that is the port, source of Boston's wealth and hence of the church being what it is.

The description naturally starts with the Stump in all its elaboration and daring. The west doorway is placed in a projection and is Decorated. Very tall west, north, and south windows, the former of eight lights, the other two of four. Then on each side two tall two-light windows with transoms, each under an ogee gable. Blank arcading over; decorated parapet. This was no doubt intended to be the bell stage and a spire to follow – exactly as at Louth. If that had been done, the length of the church would have spoken more dramatically than it does now. But hubris gripped the Bostonians, and they decided to heighten their tower. A next stage was put on, of different masonry, with thinner buttresses and with big four-light windows with transoms, wholly transparent but uncusped – an undeniable coarsening. And then, yet later, the boldest move was resolved on, the adding of the top stage, again wholly transparent, but now handled with grace as well as boldness. A highly decorated transparent parapet and turret pinnacles sending up transparent flying buttresses to an octagon. On top again a transparent parapet stepped up in the middle, and the final eight pinnacles. It is a veritable lantern, and one reason (or pretext) for building it no doubt was that it could serve as a beacon to the sailors entering the port. The exceedingly high tower was a universal ambition of the Late Middle Ages. Yet at Boston the height is excessive. One cannot overlook the fact that tier followed tier to changed plans, and if one covers with one's hand the upper stages, a more harmonious relation between church and steeple appears at once. But harmony was not the aim of an age so bent on excesses.
[LINCOLNSHIRE]

28] St Mary Magdalene, Taunton, Somerset
Tower, *c.* 1488–1514

Taunton is the proudest of a splendid series of Somerset towers, exploiting to the full the possibilities of large belfry windows, buttresses, and pinnacles.

The design of the tower is brought out to perfection by the Hammet Street approach, an eighteenth-century idea of course and quite alien to medieval conceptions. But it is only from a greater distance that one realizes to the full how capricious the contour of the tower is, with the pinnacles standing distant from the wall below the battlements, and with the whole crown projecting so that it would be top-heavy if air were not let through all its parts, the filigree battlements and the filigree top pinnacles. It is like looking through lace, an effect which one often experiences inside churches in looking at late Gothic chantry chapels, but rarely outside. Yet with all its fancies it is still very much English Perpendicular in that all major lines are kept straight, and nothing of the flowing and swelling occurs which France or Germany or Spain would have indulged in at the time. The time incidentally can be determined by wills offering money for the building of the tower. They date from 1488 to 1514.

Now in detail. The tower has set-back buttresses with attached pinnacles on three tiers and then the already mentioned very big and tall detached pinnacles set diagonally. They reach up to the bell-openings. The west front has a west doorway with big spandrels filled by defaced scenes of the legend of the Magdalen. Above is a transomed five-light window. Doorway and window are flanked by niches for images. Then follows what is unique at Taunton: three tiers of twin three-light windows with transoms and Somerset tracery. So instead of a contrast between bare wall and a blossoming out into open and ornamented forms at the bell stage, Taunton prefers an even display of its riches. The first tiers of these window stages are of about the same size, the bell stage is a good deal taller. All the windows are transomed and have Somerset tracery, below all of them run quatrefoil friezes, and all are flanked by shafts and pinnacles. In addition the transoms of the bell-openings and the windows immediately below are enriched by demi-figures of angels. Furthermore, the lower two tiers of windows carry crocketed ogee gables, above the bell-openings the whole wall is blank panelling, and then yet another quatrefoil frieze prepares for the crown. This consists of very large battlements pierced in two-storeyed arcading. At the angles stand uncommonly tall pinnacles. They have four little storeys and then a crocketed spirelet. Once again, all this is pierced. Finally to accompany battlements and pinnacles there are, corbelled out from the corners and the middle of the sides, yet thinner wholly detached shafts with pinnacles. The tower was rebuilt from the ground in 1862 by Benjamin Ferrey and Sir G. G. Scott. But the job was apparently done extremely carefully and no visual damage has come of it.
[SOUTH AND WEST SOMERSET]

29] St John Baptist, Needham Market, Suffolk
Roof, later fifteenth century

Late medieval carpenters' skills are nowhere better demonstrated than in the churches of fifteenth-century East Anglia, which were provided with roofs of an unparalleled complexity, none more so than at Needham Market, built at the expense of Bishop Grey of Ely (1458–78).

The roof is 'the climax of English roof construction' (Crossley), 'the culminating achievement of the English carpenter' (Cautley). No statements could be truer. Earl Stonham or Mildenhall may be richer and of a stronger appeal to the senses, but the intellect must give Needham Market first prize. What the carpenter has achieved here is to build a whole church with nave and aisles and clerestory seemingly in the air. The eye scarcely believes what it sees, and has a hard if worth-while job in working out how this unique effect could be attained. The roof is a hammerbeam roof with hammers coming forward a full 6 ft 6 in. The arched braces supporting them are hidden (as at Framlingham) by a boarded coving with angels with spread-out wings and fleurons. Against the ends of the hammerbeams again angels with alternately swept-upward and spread-out wings (twentieth century). There are also pendants suspended from the hammerbeams. This is done to give the impression that the chief distinguishing structural members of the Needham Market roof – the storey-posts – were not standing on the hammerbeams, but suspended from the top. They are very tall, and carry the cambered tie-beams of the low-pitched roof of the church.

But between the hammerbeams and that roof much else is happening. At the point where the arched braces meet the hammerbeams vertical so-called ashlar posts rise, as they do in any canted wagon roof of the single-frame type. And they support, again as in normal canted wagon roofs, the rafters, which reach up like lean-to roofs to the storey-posts. The posts at about one-third of their height are cross-connected, i.e. from west to east, by cambered tie-beams, and at about two-thirds of their height, i.e. just below the place where the lean-to roof reaches them, are transversely connected, i.e. from north to south, by cambered tie-beams on shallow arched braces. Finally, and this is the most astonishing feature, the upper thirds of the storey-posts are cross-connected, i.e. from west to east, by a timber-built clerestory with windows. This feature, as well as the treatment of the ashlar posts and lean-to rafters, creates the impression to which reference was made at the outset, the impression of a whole church in mid-air. The storey-posts are its piers, the rafters on the ashlar posts its aisle roofs. In addition there is plenty of decoration, even if the storey-posts remain a severely structural feature. The tie-beams are all crenellated, and the arched braces carved. Finally, apart from the aesthetic thrill there is the fact that, as Cautley says, 'this would seem to be the only open type of roof which exerts no outward thrust on the walls'.

[SUFFOLK]

82

30] St James, Swimbridge, Devon
Rood screen, late fifteenth century

In Devon (like East Anglia, one of the wealthiest areas of late medieval England), churches were less ambitious in scale, but were filled with furnishings of great richness.

Among the uncommonly lavish furnishings is one of the most glorious Devon screens: 44 ft long, right across nave and aisles, the mullions of the tracery unusually richly carved, wainscoting of unusual design with leaf decoration in all its parts, a completely preserved coving with ribs on angel corbels and panels between the ribs which have on the west side finely designed leaf and scroll motifs, not yet in the Italian taste, and on the east side coarser, broader Perpendicular motifs. The cornice a close tangle of nobbly, bossy leaf forms. Where the screen crosses the arcade an opening is left, probably for a side altar with its reredos, and above this there is a plain forward-curving coving, also with leaf panels. The one on the north side is original, the other restoration.

[NORTH DEVON]

84

31] St Peter, Chillingham, Northumberland
Monument to Sir Ralph Gray, died 1443

The taste for superabundant ornament is illustrated also in this exceptionally well preserved mid-fifteenth-century tomb with its excellent carving in alabaster, a popular material for late medieval effigies.

A sumptuous monument of considerable artistic importance, because against the tomb-chest there stand fourteen figures of saints in niches separated by figures of angels, and all these figures escaped the iconoclasts of the sixteenth and seventeenth centuries. So here is an example of dated sculpture of *c.* 1450, the date of the Beauchamp Chapel at Warwick, and although the sculptural quality of the Gray tomb is much inferior to the Earl of Warwick's the stylistic position is the same – drapery folds just breaking, though not yet as crackly as generally late in the fifteenth century. Rich, thickly encrusted canopy work. Alabaster effigies, and a background or reredos – for the head side of the tomb stands against the wall – with a standing angel and left and right two demi-figures of angels holding big helmets. Above that Jacobean addition with elaborate strapwork cartouche and obelisks.
[NORTHUMBERLAND]

32] King's College, Cambridge
Chapel, begun 1446, completed 1515

Despite its long building history, the interior of King's College chapel is a harmonious whole, a supreme achievement of a series of royal masons of the highest calibre.

One of the major monuments of English medieval architecture. The foundation stone of the chapel was laid on 25 July 1446. It is 289 ft long, 94 ft high (interior height 80 ft), and 40 ft wide. These dimensions are almost exactly those given in Henry VI's so-called Will of 1448. So the plan is primarily his and perhaps that of his resident master mason, Reginald Ely, though it may also be his London master mason's, who at the time was Robert Westerley, or any experienced advisers of his, such as William Waynflete, Bishop of Winchester. It was completed only in 1515, owing to long breaks in the execution. About the third phase (1508–15) we know most. Contracts are preserved. The master mason was John Wastell, who had been at Canterbury in the nineties and to whom can be attributed the fan-vaulted east end of Peterborough, built *c.* 1500. He made the great vault, the pinnacles of the buttresses, the angle turrets, the porches, and the vaults of all the side chapels except the two at the north-east. The master carver was Thomas Stockton.

The effect of the interior is superb. The room seems very long and very high and at the same time perfectly clear and crisp in its dimensions. It appears rich, thanks especially to the surging-up form of the conoids of the fan-vaults, but not fantastic, because most of the decoration takes the elementary form of panels. There is little solid wall, only enough on each side of the shafts to have one tall narrow panel. The uprights of these panels of the shafts, which run many-spliced up to the vault, and of the mullions of the windows dominate insistently, especially in the perspective view from the west. The fan-vaults are held down by the strong emphasis on the four-centred transverse arches, an emphasis which the most important fan-vault before King's College did not attempt: Sherborne Abbey, Dorset. So the sight above one's head is magnificent but is not without weight; it does not lose touch with the earth below.

The side chapels which fill the spaces between the buttresses do not form part of the internal picture at all. In the choir they are separated by the wall against which the choir stalls are placed, and in the nave or antechapel they are screened off. These screens may be a reminiscence of that fountain head of the Perpendicular style, Gloucester choir, or they may simply be in the accepted tradition of chantry chapels. In any case they compress the visual effect into the narrow confines of the nave.

[CAMBRIDGESHIRE]

Secular Architecture
from the late thirteenth to the early sixteenth century

Castles displayed great ingenuity in combining domestic functions with military needs. The impressive symmetry that could result contrasts with the picturesquely haphazard compositions of purely domestic buildings, although these often included vestigial defensive features such as gatehouse and battlements. Inside, the showpiece of later medieval buildings was the elaborately roofed great hall.

33] Little Wenham Hall, Suffolk
c. 1270–80

Few early manor houses have survived as unaltered as Little Wenham.

The house was built *c.* 1270–80, probably for Sir John de Vallibus and his successor Petronilla of Nerford. It is of great historical importance for two reasons. The first is that it is built of brick, and represents one of the earliest uses of home-made brick in England. Flint is used only for the base of the walls and stone for the much rebuilt buttresses and dressings. The second point of outstanding interest is that the house is a house and not a keep. It is fortified of course, but it is in its shape and appointment on the way from the fortress to the manor house and so ranks with Stokesay and Acton Burnell in Shropshire of about the same years as one of the incunabula of English domestic architecture. The house is L-shaped with a spiral staircase in the re-entrant angle. It has always stood on its own, and the only place where an attachment has existed and has disappeared is the west half of the south wall. What has disappeared is probably a garderobe.

On the first floor lie hall and chapel. The hall has four windows, all of two lights with plate tracery, including unencircled trefoils and quatrefoils. From the hall to the east one enters the chapel. East window of three lights with bar tracery of quatrefoiled circles. Above the chapel is the solar (or guard room?). This has two windows with Y-tracery on polygonal shafts. The roofs are embattled, and the different heights of hall range, chapel range, and stair-turret create a picturesque skyline.
[SUFFOLK]

34] Mayfield Palace, East Sussex
Great hall (now chapel of the Convent of the Holy Child Jesus),
early fourteenth century

Mayfield is one of the best preserved of the numerous houses of the Archbishops of Canterbury,
providing convenient country retreats between London and Canterbury.

The remains of this palace of the Archbishops of Canterbury include one of the most spectacular medieval halls of England. The hall belongs to the fourteenth century and, according to its style, the first half. It is 68 by 38 ft in size and crossed by three spectacular pointed stone arches carrying a timber roof. The arches rest on sumptuous leaf brackets which in their turn rise from busts or figures. The mouldings of the arches are of big and smaller sunk quadrants. The windows are tall, of two lights with a transom, and have cusped trefoils with ogee details in their heads and arches to the lights below the transoms. The windows are shafted to the hall. Two minor doorways at the high table end, i.e. the east end, in the south-east corner. One corner shaft serves them both. To the north of the high table is a bay-window and on the east wall (behind the archbishop's seat) an arched recess with stone diapering. High up in the same wall is a window in the form of a spherical triangle set in a blank normal window surround.
[SUSSEX]

35] Bolton Castle, Castle Bolton, North Yorkshire
Late fourteenth century

Castle building remained the obvious way to demonstrate a great magnate's power. The compact type illustrated by Bolton was a development of the fourteenth century, an alternative to the keep enclosed by curtain walls.

Bolton Castle is a climax of English military architecture. It represents a state of balance between the claims of defence, of domestic complexity and comfort, and of an aesthetically considered orderliness. The castle was built by Richard de Scrope, who obtained licence to crenellate in 1379, but had already made his contract with John Lewyn, mason, in 1378, and from the contract, which is preserved, it appears that 1378 was not the date of the start of operations either. The castle was intended to guard Wensleydale.

It belongs to the most imposing type of the fourteenth century, the type with four mighty corner towers and four ranges of living quarters round an enclosed courtyard. It is the type of Sheriff Hutton in Yorkshire, licensed in 1382, of Lumley in County Durham, licensed in 1389, and also of Bodiam in Sussex, licensed in 1386. It stands to almost full height, except for the north-east tower, and so – although it is mostly gutted inside – still gives something like the original shock of power and menace when seen from the south. The towers are of four storeys, the ranges between of three. No later age has changed the original appearance, except for the seventeenth-century windows with mullions and one transom in the west range.

[YORKSHIRE : THE NORTH RIDING]

36] Warkworth Castle, Northumberland
Late fourteenth century

Near the Scottish borders castles remained a military necessity throughout the Middle Ages; at Warkworth defensive and domestic requirements were brilliantly combined.

In 1332 Warkworth Castle was given to Henry, second Lord Percy of Alnwick. It has remained in the Percy family ever since. Its great building period came after the Scottish invasion of 1383–4. The builder was the first Earl who died in 1407 and perhaps his grandson (1416–55).

The keep is placed on the base of the higher and more pointed Norman mount. Here is one of the rare cases where the military engineer happened to be a great architect. The design of castles and bastions as a rule has nothing to do with the art of architecture. Shapes are devised for utilitarian purposes exclusively, openings are made, whether doors or windows, as safety permits. Considerations of aesthetics are as a rule completely absent. But the Warkworth keep is a work of architecture in the sense that both its mass and its inner spaces are beautiful as well as useful. It was the Edwardian engineers of the late thirteenth century who for the first time in England had raised castle building to an art capable of aesthetic effects as intense as those of churches. Harlech and Beaumaris in their crystalline shapes are as much art as the Westminster chapter house. The fourteenth century then, thanks to internal peace on the island, saw a great increase in comfort within the castle – at the expense of formality. But the formal, symmetrical plan was revived a hundred years later in such castles as Bodiam in Sussex. Warkworth is the apogee of formal design, and it proves the genius of its designer that it is at the same time a residence of considerable comfort.

The Warkworth keep is a square with bevelled edges and polygonal turrets attached to the middle of the four sides. It ends in an unembattled parapet, and above that rises a high slim turret with yet higher stair-turret. It is a shape of great clarity and force. And whereas inside the earlier keeps there are on each floor no more than two or possibly three rooms and some cells in the thickness of the walls, Warkworth has a complete system of rooms arranged so as to make sense. It is on the main floor that the composition of the rooms is so admirable and shows the resourcefulness of the architect so convincingly. The staircase in the south projection leads to an anteroom, and from there one enters the hall. The chapel fills one of the Greek cross projections, and the bevelled edges make a perfect polygonal apse. North of the chapel is another living room. This is one-storeyed and has yet another above. One may assume that the usual solar was the room above buttery and pantry, i.e. west of the hall and facing south.

From this description it will be patent how ingeniously all the comfort which a rich and powerful man might expect in his house about 1400 was provided within a keep. Yet the accommodation which the architect had designed can never have been regarded as more than subsidiary. For there were also the much larger hall and chapel in the bailey, quite apart from the new collegiate church begun probably just when the keep was begun. However, Percy knew from experience how often and how long stays within an unassailable stronghold might have to be.

[NORTHUMBERLAND]

37] Rufford Old Hall, Lancashire
Great hall, late fifteenth century

The great majority of medieval domestic buildings were of timber; heavy and elaborate roof structures such as that of Rufford were a speciality of the north-west.

Rufford Old Hall was built by the Heskeths, but that it was Robert who held the manor in 1463–90 is guesswork. The late fifteenth century anyway is, however, the most likely date, also by comparison with other timber-framed Lancashire houses, e.g. Smithills Hall, Bolton, Ordsall Hall, Salford, and Samlesbury, all of that time.

    This interior is the most overpowering of them all, of an exuberance of decoration matched nowhere else in England. Structurally you have five hammerbeam trusses of which two correspond to the bay-window, and then the spere truss characteristic of the English North. The hammerbeams have angel figures, and the arched braces lead up to collar-beams with thick bosses in their middles. In addition there are three tiers of wind-braces forming quatrefoils, and in their middles curious concave-sided square paterae. The speres are tree-trunks shaped into octagons and covered with shallowly carved small Perpendicular panels. Quatrefoils again fill in the space between speres and side walls. And in the wide space between the speres is the only originally preserved movable screen, a monster of a screen, and movable only if you accept a very optimistic meaning of the term. The framing is by moulded posts and horizontals of great size, the infilling consists of eight traceried panels, the posts are buttressed by diagonal projections coming far forward on both sides, and on top are three enormous supporters or pinnacles of barbaric shapes, the middle one so big that it has its own angel corbels on both sides. The component parts of the supporters look like ropes or scalaria shells. You will be reminded more of Indonesia than of Lancashire. The beams of the bay-window are thickly moulded too, and in the two end walls you are back at quatrefoils. Those of the high table side belong to the restoration of 1949, the other side, i.e. the screens passage side, has them original. Original also are the five doorways with four-centred heads and decorated lintels which led into kitchen, buttery, and pantry.

[NORTH LANCASHIRE]

98

38] Compton Wynyates, Warwickshire
Early sixteenth century

The medieval domestic exterior with no pretensions to a castle did not aim at symmetry; doors and windows simply reflected the irregular arrangement of traditional internal planning.

Compton Wynyates was in the olden days known as Compton-in-the-Hole, a graceless way of saying that the house lies in a hollow, with hills – low hills – rising on all sides. The house is essentially still that built by Sir William Compton early in the sixteenth century. It is the perfect picture-book house of the early Tudor decades, the most perfect in England in the specific picturesque, completely irregular mode, the very opposite to the roughly contemporary Herstmonceux, Oxburgh, or Thornbury. It is a courtyard house and originally had a moat (which was drained in the Civil War). It is of brick, partly with diapering and with just two timber-framed gables on the west or entrance side.

Take that side in detail. The porch first of all is not in the centre. It is two-storeyed, the entrance with a four-centred arch and decorated spandrel, the top with battlements. There is a projection on the left of the porch, a higher projection further out on the right. The two half-timbered gables, needless to say, do not match either. They have incidentally kept their original bargeboards. The projections and the porch, and other projections on the north and south sides, have straight joints, i.e. were added to a house with plainer frontages. The house in that form may have been of *c.* 1500. The principal projection on the south side is a big, quite irregular embattled tower, its right part recessed and higher than the rest. To the right of the tower follows the wall of the chapel with a five-light window with arched lights at the top and also below a transom. The windows immediately left and right of the chapel window are symmetrically arranged.

[WARWICKSHIRE]

39] Forde Abbey, Dorset
Hall and porch of the abbot's lodging, early sixteenth century

Sumptuous late medieval abbots' houses, such as that of the Cistercian abbey of Forde, often survived the dissolution of the monasteries, as they could easily be converted for later secular owners.

Forde Abbey was founded as a Cistercian house from Waverley in Surrey in 1136 and transferred to Forde in 1141. The building as we see it now combines the Middle Ages, chiefly the twelfth, thirteenth, and early sixteenth centuries, with work of *c*. 1650–60 carried out for Edmund Prideaux, Attorney General under Cromwell. The quality of the early sixteenth century and the Prideaux parts is among the highest in the country, and the blend is a happy one.

Of the medieval work, Perpendicular – Latest Perpendicular – without any doubt dominates. This is due to the ambition of Abbot Chard, who built himself a dwelling on a scale to justify the Reformation and the Dissolution. His princely great hall is preceded by a porch of equal pretensions. It is a tower so elaborate that it must be described motif for motif. An entrance with a basket arch leads into a fan-vaulted lobby. Above is a two-storeyed oriel, each tier with six narrow lights and a transom, though below the transom Prideaux has rationalized the display. Lozenges, shields, etc., in the sill zone, buttress shafts at the angles, a top frieze, and battlements. The porch led into the east bay of the great hall, a hall of five bays with large four-light windows with transoms and very slightly segmental tops, originally to north as well as south. Again a top frieze, and battlements. In the frieze one notices certain Renaissance motifs. So this is when the Renaissance comes in, i.e. *c*. 1525–35.
[DORSET]

Architecture and Sculpture
of the mid sixteenth century

The mid sixteenth century is a time of transition; although the art of the Italian Renaissance began to reach England from around 1520, at first it only affected ornament. The gradual understanding of the principles of classical architecture owed much to French intermediaries.

40] St Mawes Castle, Cornwall
1540–3

The coastal castles built by Henry VIII towards the end of his reign because of fear of a French invasion display a decisive break with tradition, their low, thick walls designed as mountings for cannon.

Aesthetically the trefoil leaves of the three bastions of Henry VIII's St Mawes Castle stretching out on two levels to south-west, south-east, and north-west from the taller circular centre give an impression of all-round symmetry and harmony of composition strikingly un-medieval and convincingly of the Renaissance. If one compares St Mawes with Pendennis, and with Deal, Walmer, and Camber in Kent and Sussex, all ingenious variations on the theme of the grouping of semicircular units, this impression is confirmed and enhanced. Yet these shapes were not devised for reasons of pleasure in geometrical play. They were considered by Henry VIII and his engineers (or *devisors*, as they were called) the most up-to-date fortifications. The art of defence had changed much since the Middle Ages owing to the introduction of cannon and gunpowder. Low bastions were now preferable to the high keeps and gatehouses of the past. While such work must have appeared wonderfully new and ingenious to the English, it was in fact only moderately up-to-date. Round bastions, as recommended by Dürer in his book on fortifications in 1525 and much used in Italy about and after 1500, were just then being replaced in the most modern designs of Francesco di Giorgio and Sammicheli by the angular bastion to which the future belonged.

To the visitor today the lobed shape of the terraces overlooking Falmouth Bay (the middle one larger and lower than the right and left ones) remains unforgettable, regardless of their functional qualities or shortcomings. The decorative detail also is of a high standard of craftsmanship: gargoyles, carved coats of arms, and inscriptions. The latter were devised by John Leland, the antiquary and chaplain to Henry VIII, and carried out by masons familiar with the new Renaissance fashion.
[CORNWALL]

104

41] Winchester Cathedral, Hampshire
Chantry chapel of Bishop Gardiner, died 1555

Chantry chapels, abolished by Henry VIII, were revived briefly under the Roman Catholic Queen Mary. Bishop Gardiner's is a revealing mixture of old and new artistic forms.

Bishop Gardiner died as late as 1555, and to the architectural observer the chapel tells that in a most illuminating way. The chapel is far from homogeneous. It is Gothic in parts, Early Renaissance in parts, and as early as anywhere in England High Renaissance in a few parts. The chapel front is to the north aisle not the chancel. The substructure here is entirely English mid-sixteenth-century, i.e. two fine long strapwork panels, very subdued in the details. Between them is an oblong recess, and there – very late, but still earlier than Pilon's Henri II of France – is the bishop's decomposed corpse. Above are the same purely Gothic four-light windows as in the chancel screens, but they are framed by something between buttresses and pilasters. Then, however, follows a triglyph frieze, and that in England means inspiration from the full Cinquecento, no longer from the Early Renaissance. The charming cresting on the other hand is entirely Early Renaissance. Inside, the chapel is divided into a small east sacristy and the chapel proper.

Now inside the chapel the clash of two ages is most violent. The vault is panelled in square cusped panels. Looking towards the reredos one is surprised that there is not a coffered tunnel-vault instead, such as one finds them at Chambord and over Henri II's staircase in the Louvre. For the reredos has fluted colonnettes, not decorated pilasters any longer. Such fluted columns appear so early only very rarely in England (Framlingham, Norfolk, with death dates of 1557 and 1564; Wing 1552). There are also shell-headed niches, and they are just as rare (Framlingham again; death date 1554). At the top is a proper cornice, and below a guilloche frieze. The two remaining statuettes are full Cinquecento too and have nothing left of the Gothic. How is it then that the Gothic four-light windows and even more the tiny fan-vault in the sacristy were not felt to be painfully out of date?

[HAMPSHIRE AND THE ISLE OF WIGHT]

42] All Saints, Wing, Buckinghamshire
Tomb of Sir Robert Dormer, dated 1552

This isolated example of a monument fully in the Renaissance spirit had no immediate successors.

The finest monument of its date in England and of an unparalleled purity of Renaissance elements. Sarcophagus with bucranion and two garlands. The architectural surround surprisingly wide. Coupled fluted Corinthian columns left and right on tall bases with strapwork. Against the wall coupled pilasters on bases correspond to these. The columns and pilasters carry a straight entablature elaborately detailed. The soffit has simple repeating strapwork motifs. The monument at first sight resembles north Italian work, such as Sammicheli's Bembo monument at Padua. Another comparison is with the most classical interior details of Écouen, which are, however, not earlier, but in all probability a little later. Moreover, the stone is local, and the strapwork is local too. So one should perhaps rather think of the admittedly less pure Sharington monument at Lacock Abbey in Wiltshire (1553) and thus of the circle round the Lord Protector and the Duke of Northumberland. The Duke in 1552 married the sister of Sir Robert Dormer's son's wife, Mary Sidney, and this son, Sir William, no doubt commissioned the monument.
[BUCKINGHAMSHIRE]

43] Gonville and Caius College, Cambridge
Gate of Virtue, 1567

The essentially classical concept of the triumphal gates at Caius reflects the fascination of the Renaissance world with ceremonial processions.

Dr Caius was born in 1510. He studied at Gonville Hall, was made a fellow at the age of twenty-three, and first specialized in Greek, Latin, and Hebrew. But in 1539 he went to study medicine at Padua and returned to England in 1544, after having visited Rome, Florence, and Bologna, and no doubt passed through France. He became physician to Edward VI and Queen Mary, and President of the College of Physicians. In 1556 or 1557 he made up his mind to devote his riches to the foundation of a new college at Cambridge, and chose 'that poor house now called Gonville Hall' for the purpose. He obtained a charter in 1557 and was made Master in 1559. He died in 1573.

Where Dr Caius had his fun was in the conception and probably also the design of the three gateways, which were meant to symbolize the passage of the student through the college – *per ardua ad astra*. The Gate of Humility led into a piece of open ground from which a straight path led to the Gate of Virtue. This is a much grander affair and historically one of the most important buildings of its date in England.

Broadly speaking the position was this. The Italian Renaissance had come into England as an ornamental fashion rather than an architectural style. Such it remained until the middle of the century, when a few people, guided as a rule more by the France of Lescot, Delorme, and Bullant than by the Italians, tried to achieve something purer and more comprehensive. The first move seems to have been due to the Protector Somerset and Somerset House in London (1547–52): Lacock Abbey in Wiltshire followed (*c.* 1550) and a few funeral monuments. Dr Caius's Gate of Virtue must be added to this small number. Its east side with the word 'Virtutis' is a three-bay, three-storey composition of three orders of pilasters, far from correct, but no doubt derived from Roman precedent, as illustrated by Serlio and popularized (much more classically) by Lescot and Delorme. The gateway is round-headed, and there are Victories (*à la* Sansovino) in the spandrels. Caius might have seen such Victories on Roman triumphal arches or indeed in Falconetto's town hall at Padua of 1532. His own Victories are far from handsome. The crowning motif on the centre bay is a pediment raised above an attic decorated by a curious grid of circles and lozenges and connected with the side bays by shallow curves much as in Italian church façades. All this is of a style very different from that developed at the same moment at Longleat, the style which was soon to be the Elizabethan style all over the country. The west side of the Gate of Virtue is inscribed '*Io Caius Posuit Sapientiae 1567*'. So the student had now proceeded from Humility to Virtue and from Virtue to Wisdom. Finally the Gate of Honour is reached, leading the student out of the college towards the Old Schools, where he would be given his degree.

[CAMBRIDGESHIRE]

Elizabethan and Jacobean Architecture: 1560–1620

After the Reformation church building virtually ceased for a century. Country houses of courtiers and gentry and the occasional public building provided the main vehicles for the adoption of the principles of classical symmetry in both plans and elevations. Exteriors and interior fittings were embellished by the classical orders, at first in a sober manner, but by the middle of Elizabeth's reign often with an exuberance inspired by Netherlandish pattern books.

44] Moreton Corbet Castle, Shropshire
c. 1579

The castle precinct provides the setting for this progressive example of Elizabethan architecture.

The last word has certainly not been said about this magnificent ruin. A roughly triangular enclosure with a splendid Elizabethan range along the south side, a keep of *c.* 1200 to the north of it, and a gatehouse at the north-east apex. The gatehouse was altered in 1579 (see the north window and plaque). The Elizabethan range has the date 1579 at the south-west corner and the cypher E.R. 21 (i.e. again 1579) at the south-east corner. The range was built by Sir Andrew Corbet (who died in 1579) and his sons. Sir Andrew had however built a half-range and staircase along the east wall of the enclosure a little before. Of this little survives, though old drawings tell of its four-transomed bay-window. Of the range with the date 1579 much stands upright. Architecturally it was amongst the most impressive and consistent designs in the country. It ought to rank with Kirby Hall in Northamptonshire. South front of two tall storeys, the upper taller than the lower. Both have three- to five-light windows with two transoms. The façade is articulated throughout in the French way by attached Tuscan columns (with an ornamented metope frieze) below, by slim fluted Ionic columns above, an exceptional thing in England, though one familiar from Longleat, Wiltshire. Tall slim ogee-shaped gables with pedimented windows of three lights. There is also a rhythm of flat wall and slightly projecting bays.
[SHROPSHIRE]

45] Hardwick Hall, Derbyshire

1590–9

The great aristocratic houses were often on new sites, abandoning the agglomerations of past centuries. This outstanding example can be attributed to the architect Robert Smythson, who had earlier worked at Wollaton.

Bess of Hardwick was born at Hardwick Hall. Her father, John Hardwick, Esq., owned the manor, a minor manor, and lived in a minor manor house. In 1590, after the death of her fourth husband, the sixth Earl of Shrewsbury, Bess started to build a new Hall at Hardwick, close to the old, but on virgin ground, on a grand scale, to a new, entirely up-to-date plan, and at a rate of employment that enabled her to finish the job in seven years.

Hardwick Hall is basically H-shaped in plan, like, say, Montacute in Somerset, but with a double-stepped extension at each of its shorter ends. The motif of this stepping Bess or her architect may have taken from Wollaton Hall in Nottinghamshire, completed five years before she started. There however it is used for a square not an oblong mansion. In elevation the most original feature at Hardwick is that it is of two storeys, but the projecting arms of the H and the centres of the stepped-forward additions are carried up to form three-storeyed pavilions, or square towers. That motif comes without doubt from Barlborough, also in Derbyshire, built in 1584. But whereas Barlborough has only four towers and they are polygonal and relatively slender so that their effect is rather like that of the raised turrets of Tudor gatehouses, the six towers at Hardwick are four-square and massive. Four-square is indeed the whole house. There are no curves anywhere, save in the rather niggly strapwork frills of the tower balustrades which frame Bess's proud and ostentatious initials, ES, ES, ES, ES, four times along each of the long fronts, and three times along the short ones. The stepping on the left and right moves in hard right angles, a colonnade with straight entablature runs along the ground floor between the towers of the main façades (it was originally meant to run all round the building, but the idea was given up during building), a balustrade finishes the composition at the top, the roof is flat, the central bay-window only slightly canted on the second upper floor, and all the windows are mullioned as well as transomed. 'Hardwick Hall more window than wall'; it is indeed the size and the rhythm of the windows that distinguishes Hardwick from all other Late Elizabethan houses. The close grid of the mullions and transoms sets the pace, and no obstacle gets into its way. One transom on the ground floor which is treated as a basement, two transoms on the first, three on the second and third. (The heightening from three to four tiers of panes was an afterthought, resolved on in 1593.) It is of a consistency and hardness which must have suited the old woman entirely. And as the house stands on the flattened top of the hill, there is nothing of surrounding nature either that could compete with its uncompromising, unnatural, graceless, and indomitable self-assertiveness. It is an admirable piece of design and architectural expression: no fussing, no fumbling, nor indeed any flights of fancy.

[DERBYSHIRE]

46] Triangular Lodge, Rushton, Northamptonshire
1594–7

Much thought was devoted in the Elizabethan age to the planning of gardens and garden buildings. This example perfectly illustrates the punning wit of the time with its interest in symbolism and allegory.

The Treshams were a distinguished family in Northamptonshire more than a century before the building of the Triangular Lodge at Rushton. This was the work of the Sir Thomas Tresham who was born in 1534 and knighted in 1575. He was brought up a Protestant but turned Catholic in 1580. His Catholic zeal was exceptional. He was learned in divinity and a great believer in symbols and other conceits to demonstrate his faith. Among his books and papers there was, according to the calendar of the Rushton papers, 'A Roll . . . containing figures and signs apparently working out a religious anagram upon his name and that of his Patron Saint' and also 'Some mystical notes . . . on the Trinity with a ridiculous account of a miracle which happened to him'. He was imprisoned as a Catholic in 1580 and remained confined to the Fleet and other less rigorous places till 1593. He was again in prison in 1596–7 and in 1599–1603 (or a little earlier). He died in 1605, in the same year in which Francis, his son, died in the Tower after having been involved in the Gunpowder Plot.

The Triangular Lodge stands at the north-west corner of the estate. It was begun in 1594 and completed in 1597, although the dates on the building are 1593 (date on the iron anchors of the ground floor) and 1595 (date on the chimneyshaft). The most perfect example in architectural terms of the Elizabethan love of the conceit. Everything about the little building is directed by the number three, i.e. allegorizes the Trinity. It was also a pun on Tresham's own name. The Treshams' emblem was the trefoil, and so there are plenty of trefoils on the building. But the plan and most of the details are based on the equilateral triangle. The building is of alternating bands of light and darker limestone. Its sides are 33 ft 4 in. long, i.e. one third of a hundred. There are three storeys, each with three windows in each of the three sides. The principal room on each floor is a hexagon. The corner spaces are triangular. One contains the newel staircase, the others small rooms. The basement windows are small trefoils on all sides with a smaller triangle in the centre of each. On the raised ground floor the south-east side has a very narrow entrance which has the figures 5555 written on the lintel and a very odd steep gable consisting of short straight sides and two-thirds of a circle standing on them. On each side there are three gables with crockets, triangular top obelisks, emblems, and inscriptions. Among the emblems are the seven-branched candelabra, the seven eyes of God, and the Pelican.

What does all this amount to? A folly? A bauble? A pretty conceit? It cannot be treated so lightly. It is no more nor less than a profession of faith in stone – of a faith for which Tresham spent more than fifteen years in prison and confinement. So one should look at the Triangular Lodge with respect.

[NORTHAMPTONSHIRE]

47] Schools Quadrangle, Oxford
Frontispiece, 1613–24

The gate tower is a late medieval type; here it has been brought up to date by a magnificent piece of classical oneupmanship.

It was due to the energy and liberality of Sir Thomas Bodley that a new library for the University of Oxford was got together and made usable. Bodley had been a Fellow of Merton, lecturer in Greek and Hebrew, and the Queen's Ambassador in the Netherlands in 1589–96. The Schools Quadrangle, considering its date, 1613–24, is a formidable building and without parallel in the secular architecture of those years. The conception, one speculates, may have been less the master masons' – John Akroyd of Halifax (who had worked at Merton in 1609 and died in 1613) and John Bentley (who died in 1615) – than Bodley's, although only the second floor was built for his purposes and the rest indeed for the Schools.

    After passing through the main archway into the quad, one should turn back at once, for such a frontispiece as this one will never see again. With five tiers it is the biggest in England, and that means anywhere. The *parti* of these frontispieces is of course Italo-French Renaissance in origin, and from France Lord Protector Somerset had taken it over for Somerset House and then William Cecil for Burghley House, Robert Cecil for Hatfield House – dated 1612 – and so on. Few have more than three tiers – Stonyhurst in the 1590s e.g. has four. Bodley's starts with a plain stage of coupled Tuscan columns. Next slim Roman Doric pairs, with a broad band of mixed strap and foliage motifs also round the pedestals of the columns. In addition the columns have their lower two-fifths decorated. Six-light, transomed window. Top frieze of strapwork. Next stage Ionic columns with decorated plinths; six-light window with two transoms. Next stage Corinthian columns, and between them a big panel showing James I seated in a niche under a canopy which, taking in the niche, is round in plan, and to his left Fame, to his right the kneeling University. Above and reaching into the top stage three statuettes. Composite columns with strapwork plinths and frieze, and another six-light window. The polygonal angle turrets end in crocketed spires, and between them is a big pierced strapwork cresting.

[OXFORDSHIRE]

48] Langleys, Great Waltham, Essex
Dining room, with plasterwork of *c.* 1620, restored after 1711

Decorative plasterwork, often executed with great inventiveness, was used to give all-over enrichment to Jacobean overmantels and ceilings.

The house is mostly early-eighteenth-century, but incorporating in the north wing much of a preceding house of *c.* 1620. The library and the old dining room display plasterwork of an exuberance not exceeded anywhere in the country. The library ceiling is vaulted, the dining-room ceiling flat. Both have patterns made by broad bands. The bands are adorned with fine trails of foliage, the spaces between them with strapwork cartouches and coats of arms, etc. As the rooms are not high, the effect is almost oppressively rich. The fireplaces in both rooms are yet more ornate, in the dining room with figures of Peace and Plenty. The mantelshelves rest on elaborate termini caryatids.

Samuel Tufnell, who bought the house in 1711, must have liked all this Jacobean splendour, for not only did he not destroy it, but he seems even to have restored and altered it in a style intended to be neo-Jacobean. The eighteenth-century work is noticeable in the pieces put in to reduce the size of the fireplace openings, and also perhaps some other details which only detailed study could ascertain. In any case, side by side with Vanbrugh's neo-Jacobean at Audley End, Mr Tufnell's must be of the earliest in England.

[ESSEX]

Mature Classicism:
1620–1700

Inigo Jones revolutionized English architecture by demonstrating the importance of proportion in classical design and by using a consistent vocabulary of forms, derived from antique models and from the sixteenth-century Italian master Andrea Palladio. Not all his contemporaries understood the significance of Jones's revolution. After the Restoration in 1660 a new generation of designers, led by Wren, applied Jones's lessons with growing confidence and freedom, and drew on their own experience of modern Dutch and French buildings.

49] Queen's Chapel, St James's Palace, London
1623–7 by Inigo Jones

Inigo Jones's pure classicism was first introduced at the Whitehall Banqueting House of 1619–22. Here he had in mind a particular antique building, the Temple of Venus and Rome.

Not being open to visitors except for services, the Queen's Chapel is not as famous as it ought to be. Not only is it one of the few certain works of Inigo Jones, it is also the first church in England built in complete opposition to the habits of the Perpendicular Gothic, which in ecclesiastical architecture had lingered on through the sixteenth century and were – as a survival or revival – to linger on through the seventeenth century, until Wren appeared. But the Queen's Chapel is unhesitatingly and uncompromisingly classical, and it is furthermore of a simplicity and beauty rarely matched in the more ingenious and complex designs of Wren. It was begun in 1623 and mostly built in 1626–7. It was from the beginning a Catholic chapel, and a friary of Capuchins was installed in St James's Palace to serve it. It has a broad Venetian window at the east end, the first, it seems, in England. The interior is dominated by the splendid wooden white and gold coffered vault, an elliptical vault incidentally, which, from the Italian point of view, is the one inconsistency in the building. There is a richly detailed cornice below it. It need hardly be said how fundamentally different this opulence of classical detail and this reposefulness are from the restless Jacobean ribbed panelled ceilings or open timber roofs. The walls of the Queen's Chapel are plain above and panelled in timber below. Most of this panelling belongs to the furnishings of the 1660s and 70s. Of Wren's time also is the gallery at the east end, the stalls and lectern, the organ gallery on the south side, and such details as the cherub and garlands in a blank south niche and the achievement and garlands above the east window (probably by Gibbons).
[LONDON I: THE CITIES OF LONDON AND WESTMINSTER]

50] Kew Palace (The Dutch House), Kew Gardens, Richmond-upon-Thames, London

1631

Virtuoso brickwork was a mid-seventeenth-century speciality, normally with coarse and carefree classical details.

Kew Palace, or the Dutch House, built in 1631 by Samuel Fortrey (a London merchant of Dutch descent) as a country house close to the river, is of the moderate size of 70 ft length and 50 ft depth. The palace is of brick, laid with supreme skill and artistry in Flemish not English bond, something of an innovation at the time. Three storeys, with to the main fronts three gables with double-curved sides and crowning pediments alternately triangular and segmental – also still an innovation in 1630. The windows originally had brick crosses of a mullion and a transom, and that was a relatively novel motif too.

The style of Kew Palace seems to have appealed to only a limited stratum of civilization: the connoisseurs and virtuosi appreciated the classicity of Inigo Jones, but the wealth of the provinces still went into buildings in the Tudor tradition, of stone in the North, timber-framed in the West. In and around London however there was a class, chiefly merchants, who scorned the Tudor tradition as old-fashioned, but could not make themselves accept the restraint of the Palladian style. For them such brick houses were built, their gables demonstrating by their crowning pediments their awareness of the Renaissance. The chief survivals of this style in the London area are Cromwell House, Highgate (*c.* 1637–40) and Swakeleys near Uxbridge (*c.* 1630–8). Broome Park, Kent (1635–8) is another contemporary example. Kew Palace is the oldest firmly dated survival (although the style appears to have been introduced to London somewhat earlier, see the pedimented gable of Lady Cooke's house in Holborn, drawn by John Smythson in 1619).

One of the most characteristic features of the house is the evident delight in play with brickwork, such as the rustication round all windows. The centre bay is enriched by super-imposed pilasters and, on the top floor, by columns – the pilasters on the ground floor have been removed – and by arched windows.

[LONDON 2 : SOUTH]

51] St Mary, East Knoyle, Wiltshire
Plaster decoration in the chancel, 1639

The beautifying of churches promoted by Archbishop Laud in the 1630s was condemned by the Puritans as tending to Popery.

The plaster decoration of the chancel is a surprise and a delight. You see Jacob's Dream on the east wall with the angels ascending and descending ladders, you see remains of an Ascension of Christ on the west wall, on the south wall the Sacrifice of Isaac, and on the north wall a kneeling man below a dove and the verse: Oh that I had wings of a dove, added to which απτερος and αποτερος. Many more verses and inscriptions. Also Jacobean-looking strapwork, in bold forms, and fine decidedly Gothic-looking vertical friezes of little intersected arches. All this is interesting enough iconographically and aesthetically, 'a strange and quaint performance', as Colt Hoare writes. What makes it twice as exciting is that the scheme was worked out by Dr Wren, Rector of East Knoyle from 1623. Christopher Wren was born at East Knoyle in 1632. Dr Wren lost his living in the Civil War, and during his trial this scheme of plasterwork was held against him. The trial was in 1647; the plasterwork was eight years old then; so it can be dated 1639.
[WILTSHIRE]

126

·I·KINGS·VERSE·3
THE LORD SAYD I HAVE
HALOWED THIS HOWSE TO
PVT MY NAME THERE
·ESAY·LVI·VERSE·7·
MY HOWSE SHALBE CALLED
THE HOWSE OF PRAYER
TO ALL NATIONS
·I·PET·II·VERSE·5
YEE ALSO AS LIVING STONES
ARE BVILT VP A SPIRITVAL HOVSE

52] St Stephen Walbrook, London
1672–9 by Christopher Wren

Wren rebuilt almost fifty London parish churches after the Fire of 1666. St Stephen has the most architecturally sophisticated interior of them all.

The most majestic of Wren's parish churches, and in at least one essential point a try-out for St Paul's. The church appears at first longitudinal and of classical composition, ending, one can see, round the altar, with just such another bay as that in which one is standing. A number of slender Corinthian columns accompany that procession on the left and right. They are all of the same height – that is, the church is of the hall-church type. It consists, we can read at once, in this west part, of a nave with oblong groin-vaulted bays, aisles with square flat-ceilinged bays, and narrow outer aisles. But almost at once it becomes clear that the church is in fact not simply longitudinal, but leads to a splendidly dominating dome with a lantern to let light in from above (reconstructed in 1951–2). It is this ambiguity between two interpretations of the space within what is really no more than a perfectly plain parallelogram that connects St Stephen with the international Baroque, in spite of Wren's English insistence on the cool and isolated columns and on classical decoration.

The spatial ambiguity does indeed go much further, for, once the dome is reached, one sees that the church can also be understood in quite a different way – as a central building with a dome on eight arches of which four arches form the introduction to cross arms of equal height and, it seems at the first moment, equal length. The transepts are actually a little shorter than the chancel. They come to an end very soon against the walls of the outer parallelogram. And the nave consists of course of two bays, not of one. But the interaction of cross and dome – two central motifs – is all the same as potent a spatial effect as the interaction of longitudinal and central. That Wren wanted this double meaning is clear for instance from the way in which the chancel has the same groined vaulting as the nave, but the transepts are tunnel-vaulted.

The next complication concerns the fact that the dome rises over a square space. That in itself is nothing unusual, and in Italy and France pendentives would have been used as a connecting motif. But Wren wished his dome to stand not on solid piers but on slender columns. So instead of one pier in each corner he has three columns in each corner, spaced so as to make the corner clear as a corner. It is in point of fact only at the level of the entablature that the whole ingenuity of all this comes to life. The columns carry a straight entablature, and this traces for us first the length of the nave on the left and right (and in the east parts of course of the chancel), then turns and marks the corners of the central span, and then turns again to run to the left and right of the transepts against the north and south walls. And now what happens above the entablature? Here again a motif of Baroque ambiguity is used to reach the circular base of the dome. The four arches of nave, chancel, and transepts Wren had available without difficulty, but he needed four more of the same height and width in the diagonals, and to obtain these he threw arches diagonally across his corners. So below the arch the result is a triangular space, and Wren covered it with a half-groin-vault. All this is clearly in the spirit of St Paul's Cathedral.

[LONDON I : THE CITIES OF LONDON AND WESTMINSTER]

53] Trinity College, Cambridge
Library, 1676–90 by Christopher Wren

This mature masterpiece by Wren is the finest college library at either of the ancient universities.

Nevile's Court is closed by Sir Christopher Wren's library, the building which introduced his mature style to Cambridge. It is 150 ft long, built of Ketton stone with its lovely variety of cream and pink hues. To the west, facing the river, the ground floor has three mighty doorways with huge attached Tuscan columns carrying straight entablatures and blank horizontal panels, surprisingly low, above (as to the reasons for this, *see* below). Between the doorways are five plus five small windows. The ground floor is thus kept well closed and solid to serve as a base for the upper floor with its large, evenly arched library windows. These are identical on both sides of the building. The east front has an open arched ground floor whose height is chosen to match the old ranges of Nevile's Court – not their ground floor, but their first floor. The arches rest on solid piers in front of which rise tall Tuscan columns, the size of those of the west doorways. These carry a Doric frieze with metopes and triglyphs.

Since, however, the internal arrangements of the library made it desirable to have windows starting well above the bookcases, Wren chose an expedient which would have been hateful to any truly classical designer. He filled the tympana of the arches in, placed his floor behind them, and thus gained his bookcase space behind the Doric frieze and the sill-zone of the windows. This conflict between external and internal arrangement, not noticed by many, is a typically Baroque feature. He took it over from Paris. The upper floor has the same windows as on the west side, large and arched, and divided by stone mullions and a transom at the height of the springing of the arch. The windows are separated by attached Ionic columns. The cornice carries a balustrade with four standing figures (Divinity, Law, Physic, Mathematics; by Cibber) above the middle columns.

The library must have come as a revelation to Cambridge, still used to such fundamentally unclassical buildings as Pepys Building at Magdalene College and Third Court at St John's. Here was sonorous grandeur, without any bragging, simplicity and ease combined with a mastery of the Romance idiom (more French in detail than Italian, although the shadow of Sansovino's library at Venice looms in the background). It made everything built to that day look fussy and finicky.

[CAMBRIDGESHIRE]

54] Hanbury Hall, Hereford and Worcester

1701

Shortly after the Restoration a style for country houses crystallized which persisted until the early eighteenth century.

As you approach the house through its grounds you will be struck by the perfect Englishness of the picture which offers itself. It is a substantial house, eleven bays wide and two storeys high, of brick with stone dressings and a central cupola. It could be in no other country. The façade is handsomely articulated by somewhat projecting three-bay wings and by a pedimented three-bay centre flanked by rather tightly placed giant columns on high pedestals. The inscribed date 1701 is no surprise. This is clearly the Wren age, and the carved decoration with volutes round the middle window is as clearly *circa* 1700. It even suggests the name of an architect, Talman. This is a guess. The similarities are with Talman's Thoresby, Nottinghamshire, in the first place, and also Chatsworth, Derbyshire, both Talman's east front, and the west front begun in 1700, and with Talman's work at Drayton, Northamptonshire, of 1702. Actually a name is recorded for Hanbury Hall: William Rudhall of Henley-in-Arden, who signed the drawings of the house which are still kept there and have different details (the columned centre only one bay wide, the pediment segmental, and more decoration), but it is unlikely that he was more than the builder. The house was built for Thomas Vernon, who was a barrister. Of further features of the façade the elegantly framed windows and the porch with Corinthian columns are all that needs a mention.

[WORCESTERSHIRE]

English Baroque:
1700–1735

Nicholas Hawksmoor, Wren's chief assistant, and John Vanbrugh, an amateur architect of genius, created a highly individual style, grandiloquent and imaginative in the arrangement of masses and the handling of space. This constitutes a delayed English response to the Italian Baroque of Bernini and Borromini. The originality of English Baroque can be seen in a series of major country houses, of which Blenheim Palace is the largest, and in the London churches built under the Act of 1711.

55] St Mary-le-Strand, London
1714–17 by James Gibbs

Gibbs's early masterpiece draws its inspiration both from Wren and from Baroque Rome, where the architect had received his training.

Rebuilt on a new site under the Act for the Fifty New Churches. Admirably placed on an island site in the Strand, and visible from all sides, as if it were a casket one can handle with one's hands. Indeed all sides are treated with loving care, the east end, in its composition, taken from St Paul's Cathedral, but in its slenderness and the daintier detail, such as the long, fine garlands hanging down left and right of the apse window, in quite a different mood. The sides of the north and south are of seven bays, in two orders, also as at St Paul's. But the orders are columns and the fact that pediments of alternating shape crown the upper order in bays two, four, and six and stand out against the top balustrade adds a livelier, much more diversified rhythm. The ground floor has banded rustication and playful little niches in the bays, the upper floor Venetian windows appearing as if behind the front layer of the columns.

The centre of the west front carries a pediment, and immediately behind this the tower goes up – a motif lacking in structural logic but one that became very popular. It was not intended at the beginning. Gibbs's plan had been for a column and a statue of Queen Anne in front of the west end. Above the clock stage is an oblong stage with detached columns to the north and south only carrying a slight entablature. Then follow some pretty bits of decoration, and then a similar motif smaller and less high, and on top of this a slim concave-sided top stage on which the little lantern is perched.

[LONDON I: THE CITIES OF LONDON AND WESTMINSTER]

56] Beningbrough Hall, North Yorkshire
Entrance hall, completed 1716 by William Thornton

This spatial drama is inspired by the hall at Castle Howard, the building which introduced so many of the distinguishing features of English Baroque.

Beningbrough Hall was built for John Bourchier and, according to a date in the parquet of the main staircase, must have been complete in 1716. The house was designed by William Thornton, a joiner-architect who died in 1721 and worked with or under Hawksmoor at Beverley Minster in 1716–20. The interiors on the main floors are both grand and delicate. They are nowhere over-emphatic nor even over-crowded. The entrance hall runs through both floors and has giant Corinthian scagliola pilasters on a high dado, arches left and right leading into Vanbrughian corridors, balconies with delicious wrought-iron railings above them looking down on the hall from upper corridors, a massive and majestic Vanbrughian fireplace with fat corbels and a curving-up frieze, and a coved ceiling with penetrations for the various arches cutting into the cove.
[YORKSHIRE: THE NORTH RIDING]

57] Seaton Delaval Hall, Northumberland
1719–29 by John Vanbrugh

The vigour and dynamism of English Baroque is nowhere expressed with such concentration as here.

Seaton Delaval was built by Sir John Vanbrugh for Admiral George Delaval. Vanbrugh was over fifty when he designed the house; the admiral was yet older, and both died before the completion of the building which was the triumph of both. No other Vanbrugh house is so mature, so compact and so powerful, and the admiral, we know from one of Vanbrugh's letters, was 'not disposed to starve the design at all'.

The plan is Palladian, that is the plan customary for villas on the Venetian *terra ferma*: a square symmetrically planned *corps de logis*, arcades to the left and right, breaking forward at an angle of ninety degrees and running along the fronts of two service wings to end by the road in small square pavilions. The forecourt or *cour d'honneur* is 180 ft deep and 152½ ft wide; the house itself is comparatively small – only about 75 by 75 ft, though with attached towers and turrets.

Now for towers and turrets one would look in vain in Palladio's serene villas, and Vanbrugh's elevations indeed utterly contradict the plan. If they are reminiscent of any Italian designer, only Piranesi's name would come to mind, and Piranesi was born a year after work had started at Seaton Delaval. What Piranesi has in common with Vanbrugh is the passion for the cyclopic, and also the theatrical, and the scorn for homely comforts. Wren, older by one generation, had a much nicer sense of when the grand manner and when a more domestic style was appropriate, Lord Burlington and his protégés, younger by one generation, a more refined and even manner. So even indeed was the strictly Palladian style which Colen Campbell and Lord Burlington had introduced about 1715 that it is not easy to keep apart in one's mind the various villas and country houses of the Burlingtonians. But no one can forget Seaton Delaval. For though it betrays the hand of its master in every detail, it is yet completely individual, with its own unique composition and mood. In details and mood it was out of date in England when it was built; for Palladianism became the fashion as soon as Lord Burlington had launched it; and perhaps Palladianism was more English than the fantasies of the English descendant of Flemish forebears.

Compared with the work of the Palladians, Seaton Delaval seems forceful and aggressive all the way through. Added diagonally to the four corners are polygonal turrets of clearly medieval ancestry, and added to the centre of the east and west sides are oblong stair towers raised higher than the turrets and façades. But the level of the tops of these towers is kept for that of the pedimented centres of both façades, and this is carried as a temple roof across from north to south. Alternating bands of bulgily raised rustication are applied to the whole ground floor and first floor of the stair towers, and in addition the house rests on a half-sunk base of yet more thickly bulging rusticated bands. The smooth to Vanbrugh evidently meant the unstressed.

[NORTHUMBERLAND]

58] Castle Howard, North Yorkshire
Mausoleum in the park, 1729–36 by Nicholas Hawksmoor,
terrace walls 1737–42 by Daniel Garrett

The antique circular temple undergoes a Baroque transformation for expressive purposes.

The mausoleum designed by Nicholas Hawksmoor was finished only in 1742, i.e. after his death. It is enormous in size and extremely noble in design, of a majestic simplicity not to be expected from the architect of St Mary Woolnoth and St George in the East. In size and cost it compares with a Wren church in the City of London. The ample double staircase, formed after the pattern of Lord Burlington's Chiswick villa, is an amendment suggested by Sir Thomas Robinson, who incidentally saw to it that Burlington himself inspected the design for the mausoleum and who was upset by Hawksmoor's key motif of the narrow spacing of the twenty columns round the cylindrical core. The Palladians were right when, in 1732, they protested. In spite of Hawksmoor's learned rejoinder referring to Vitruvius and ancient Roman monuments, his is a solecism. But it adds just that virility which distinguishes this rotunda from conventional ones in other people's gardens. The circular core has two tiers of arched niches, four of them in all glazed as windows. The columns are of the Tuscan kind, but uncommonly slender and with a triglyph frieze. Recessed drum with square windows and shallow dome. The shape of the dome, seen at a distance, is also miraculously right. A little higher, i.e. a little more Bramantesque, and it would lose the building much of its force.

[YORKSHIRE: THE NORTH RIDING]

Palladian and Gothick:
1715–1775

Reaction against English Baroque resulted in a rule of taste of which Lord Burlington set himself up as the principal arbiter. From Inigo Jones, Palladio and the architecture of antiquity a set of accepted models was formulated by the 'Palladians'. The imagination of William Kent, Burlington's principal protégé, however saved Palladianism from absolute conventionality. It was Kent too who popularized the light-hearted evocation of medieval architecture, soon taken up with more scholarship by amateurs like Horace Walpole and popularly known today as 'Gothick'.

59] Assembly Rooms, York
1730–2 by Richard Boyle, third Earl of Burlington

Early Georgian public buildings rarely aimed at grandeur. Burlington achieved it here in his literal realization of an antique room.

Richard Boyle, third Earl of Burlington, of Burlington House, Piccadilly, and Chiswick had Yorkshire property and spent time fairly regularly at Londesborough. He designed the York Assembly Rooms in 1730 and made it a serious reconstruction of what Vitruvius describes as the Egyptian Hall. The directors of the Assembly Rooms had written to him: 'We entirely leave to your lordship to do in what manner you shall think proper', and they recorded on the foundation stone that it was the design of 'Lord Burlington, the Maecenas of our age'. Defoe on the other hand called him 'surely the most tasteless Vitruvius'. The hall itself is 112 by 40 by 40 ft, and has on all sides Corinthian columns painted brownish-yellow and marbled, eighteen by six of them. Clerestory lighting with pilasters and a garland frieze. The whole is festive yet nobly restrained by operating with a minimum of motifs.
[YORKSHIRE: YORK AND THE EAST RIDING]

60] Temple of British Worthies, Stowe, Buckinghamshire
1735 by William Kent

The landscape garden was one of the outstanding achievements of Georgian culture. Buildings often had a crucial role to play, especially in the early gardens.

The view across the Elysian Fields and the lake is to the Temple of British Worthies, one of the most original conceptions and designs of the Stowe *ensemble*. It is by Kent and of 1735. It consists of a semicircle with as its centre a stepped pyramid with a very odd horseshoe-shaped empty recess. In the recess was originally a Mercury, as the god who leads souls to Elysium – apparently British as well as Grecian. Along the semicircle and at its end, i.e. facing us as we approach, are eight low niches on either side. They contain busts. Each bust is in a bay slightly projected on its own and with its own pediment. In the niches are eight busts made by Rysbrack by 1731 for Gibbs's former Belvedere and eight made for Kent's new building in 1735, either by Rysbrack or by Scheemakers. The first eight are Queen Elizabeth, Shakespeare, Bacon, Milton, Hampden, Newton, Locke, and William III (in Roman dress). The others are King Alfred, the Black Prince, Gresham, Sir John Barnard, Drake, Raleigh, Inigo Jones, and Pope. The whole is an eminently significant demonstration of national pride versus the worship of antiquity, and also interesting for the 'historicism' demonstrated in the care for accurate costume.
[BUCKINGHAMSHIRE]

144

61] 44 Berkeley Square, London
Staircase, 1742–4 by William Kent

The Palladians, for all their reliance on precedent, had their moments of dramatic originality.

No. 44 Berkeley Square might well be called the finest terrace house of London. Kent built it in
1742–4 for Lady Isabella Finch. The exterior does not tell much of what splendour he has given
the interior. Inside are the grandest staircase and the grandest drawing room of any eighteenth-
century private house in London. The staircase is fitted into an area with a square core and two
semicircular apses. The staircase itself starts in the middle, runs up to a landing in one apse, and
then returns in two curved arms to the first floor. Here the other apse is hidden by a brilliantly
Baroque screen of Ionic columns curving back in the centre. Behind the screen is the staircase
from the first to the second floor. The second-floor landing is a bridge above the screen with the
same Baroque shape. The well is glazed only above one apse. The whole is a conception of great
spatial ingenuity, executed with self-confidence. There is no other eighteenth-century staircase in
England which can so convincingly be compared with those of the great German and Austrian
Baroque architects. Horace Walpole called it a 'beautiful piece of scenery'.
[LONDON I : THE CITIES OF LONDON AND WESTMINSTER]

62] 41 Gay Street and The Circus, Bath, Avon
c. 1740 and 1754–8 respectively, both by John Wood the Elder

Bath, the fullest expression of Palladian town-planning, owed much to Wood's vision of a modern successor to Roman Aquae Sulis.

Gay Street is the work of the elder Wood, continued unnoticeably by the younger Wood. Still by the elder Wood is the corner house, No. 41, built by the great architect for himself *c.* 1740. Architects have a way of designing for themselves at a higher pitch than for clients. Wood's house, unless one wishes to discount it as a piece of advertising, is an object lesson in the divergences between an architect's desires and his executed work. Wood's severe Palladianism disappears here, and a heavy but gay Baroque takes its place. The walls, it is true, are quite plain, but at the corner is a semicircular slightly recessed bow-window designed emphatically to break the staid uniformity of the newly built streets. Ground-floor windows with heavy Gibbs surrounds, first floor with pairs of even more heavily intermittently blocked pairs of Ionic columns, plain attic storey.

Gay Street runs straight into the Circus, or the King's Circus, as it was originally called. It dates from 1754–8 and it is the most monumental of the elder Wood's works, even more so if one remembers that the old plane trees which are now so much more splendid than the buildings did not exist and were not projected. The centre was paved – stone and no greenery. Planting was introduced early in the nineteenth century. Wood's architectural conception is original and powerful. A circus so closed to the outer world is something very different from the *rond-points* of the French such as Louis XIV's Place des Victoires. Moreover, the architecture is designed so as to close the circle yet more tightly. The uninterrupted architraves are like the hoops of a barrel. The Circus has one architectural motif only, and this is relentlessly carried through on all sides – without accents of height or relief – a triumph of Wood's economy of means. The system is easily described: coupled columns in three orders, Tuscan (with metope frieze), Ionic, Corinthian, and then a top parapet. The sustained depth of relief was something new for Bath.
[NORTH SOMERSET AND BRISTOL]

148

63] Arbury Hall, Warwickshire
Dining room, *c.* 1771–9 by Henry Keene, plasterer G. Higham

The incongruity of recreating in stucco the forms of medieval masonry vaults did not worry Horace Walpole or the builder of Arbury, Sir Roger Newdigate.

Arbury Hall is one of the finest examples of the early Gothic Revival in England – some may say *the* finest, and the finest in England of course implies anywhere. Sir Roger Newdigate started gothicizing the house about 1748, almost to the year that Horace Walpole started at Strawberry Hill, kept at it longer, and in any case could work on a larger scale. From 1762 onwards Henry Keene, Surveyor to Westminster Abbey and busy at Oxford too, was in charge.

The south front centrepiece with the dining room within dates from *c.* 1771–9. The plasterer was G. Higham. By 1796, i.e. after nearly forty years, Sir Roger Newdigate could sit back and enjoy his completed house. As for the designing, it is so much of a piece throughout the principal rooms that he must have had a say himself, possibly just by suggesting sources of inspiration, but possibly also by sketching. He was capable of doing that, and drawings of his do in fact exist.

The unifying features at Arbury are great elaboration and consistent finesse of execution inside as well as outside, and a sustained preference for the Late Perpendicular of such regal buildings as Henry VII's Chapel in Westminster Abbey and the Divinity School at Oxford.

The dining room has a very large chimneypiece in the back wall, the overmantel decorated with a row of little niches projecting triangularly. In the walls are tall canopied Gothic niches (as at Lacock in Wiltshire), and in them casts of ancient Roman statues. Similarly the relief framed by the elaborate Gothic surround in the east wall is an ancient Roman relief of Bacchus. Below the relief is a later Roman sarcophagus front. Both were brought from Rome by Sir Roger. That he could still mix the classical piece with his Gothic decoration shows that he belonged to the first generation of the Gothicists. His Gothic, like Horace Walpole's, is gay, amusing, pretty – not at all venerable, as Gothic architecture is for us and has been ever since the Romantics.
[WARWICKSHIRE]

Neo-classicism:
1760–1820

In the mid eighteenth century English architecture, for the first time since the end of the Middle Ages, joined the main stream of European developments. Englishmen in Italy and Greece took a lead in rediscovering a much wider range of antique architecture and decoration than had been known to the Renaissance. The writings of the French Abbé Laugier and the German J. J. Winckelmann and the polemic of the Italian Giambattista Piranesi all had a profound effect on English art and architecture.

64] Osterley Park House, Isleworth, Hounslow, London
Remodelled from 1763 by Robert Adam

The lightness of the Rococo was recaptured by Robert Adam and others in a neo-classical idiom during the 1760s after renewed attention to the antique buildings of Italy and what remained of their decoration.

The unforgettable feature of Osterley Park, the portico, belongs to the first stage of Robert Adam's work, that is the 1760s. The detail may be due to Wood's recent publication of the Temple of Bel at Palmyra, but the basic idea is wholly Adam's, the idea of using the motif of the antique temple façade in so utterly unantique a manner. Greek and Roman front porticoes are always placed against solid walls, the columns standing out like the figures of a frieze in high relief. Robert Adam with his delight in transparency opens the whole centre of the east front by a double portico at the head of a wide staircase, thus boldly connecting outer space and inner courtyard space. The effect with the slim unfluted Ionic columns is as delicate and celestial and as chastely theatrical as any opera Gluck might have composed in these very same years.
[MIDDLESEX]

152

65] Newby Hall, North Yorkshire
Sculpture gallery, *c.* 1770–80 by Robert Adam

A gentleman who made the Grand Tour in Italy might come home with a collection of antique sculptures. Adam, recalling Hadrian's villa at Tivoli, here created an appropriate setting.

Robert Adam's interiors at Newby are amongst the finest of their date anywhere in Europe. They were carried out for William Weddell, rich virtuoso and collector of antique sculpture. The Adam wing with its superb procession of three apartments is devoted to Mr Weddell's statuary. The first and third rooms are oblong, the middle one round with niches in the corners, on the pattern of ancient Roman plans in palaces, baths, etc. At the far end of the third room is instead of a window a shallow niche. There are also smaller niches in this and the first room to take statues. The ceilings are delicately stuccoed, the vaults and covings coffered. The rotunda has a glazed eye in the dome. The colour scheme is white and pale salmon-pink.
[YORKSHIRE: THE WEST RIDING]

66] Shire Hall, Chelmsford, Essex
1789–91 by John Johnson, Surveyor to the County

Palladian compositions survived, with certain refinements, into the neo-classical period.

A thoroughly civilized public building, spurred probably by Adam's for Hertford a few years before and indeed considerably superior. Five-bay width only, but generous spacing and good Portland stone. The three middle bays project slightly and have arched entrances. The whole ground floor is rusticated. Above in the middle four attached giant columns with Adam capitals. The windows between them have pediments. The outer windows are tripartite and segment-arched. Then above the middle windows three relief-plaques (by the elder Bacon, executed in Coade stone) and a pediment. No unusual motifs or peculiarities of handwriting, but a very refined handling of familiar material.

[ESSEX]

67] St James, Great Packington, Warwickshire
1789–90 by Joseph Bonomi

The use of stumpy primitive Greek Doric columns was a sign of advanced neo-classical taste.

If one were to name the most important and the most impressive English church of the ending eighteenth century, Great Packington would be the first to come to mind. Moreover, here is the one building in England, not by Soane, which deserves to be grouped with designs by Ledoux in France and Gilly in Prussia. Moreover Great Packington church dates from 1789–90, which makes it earlier than any of Gilly's. Joseph Bonomi for the sake of this one church deserves to be a household word of English architecture, which he is not. He was born in 1739 and died in 1808. He studied in Rome, first at the Collegio Romano, and came to London in 1767. In 1784 he was back in Italy, and it is on that journey that he must have visited Paris as well; for he appears fully conversant with the style of Boullée and Ledoux. It is true that some of this he may already have picked up from the students at the Académie de France in Rome before 1767, but direct acquaintance with Paris must be assumed. Great Packington church is square, on the quincunx or inscribed-cross plan, with a square centre, four short arms, and four lower corner rooms. That is a Byzantine scheme, but one which, via Venice and Holland, Sir Christopher Wren had picked up. So Bonomi might have known it from Wren's St Anne and St Agnes in London as much as from Italy.

After the rudely utilitarian, completely and totally unornamented exterior, the interior is overwhelming. It is all faced in smooth, painted ashlar stone, walls as well as vaults. The centre vault and the corner vaults are groined, the arms tunnel-vaulted between broad, entirely unmoulded transverse arches. But set in the corners of the centre, as if to carry the vault, are four rose-coloured sandstone columns, and they are of the Greek Doric order, excessively sturdy, with an excessive entasis and weighed down by a piece of triglyph frieze. Now there were scarcely half a dozen architects in Europe in 1789 who would have had the courage to use the Greek Doric, i.e. the rudest, most elemental order. Ledoux was one of them, Gilly another, Soane a third.
[WARWICKSHIRE]

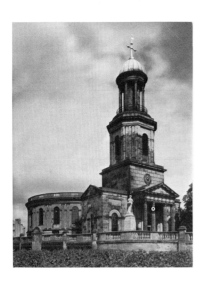

68] St Chad, Shrewsbury, Shropshire
1790–2 by George Steuart

The circular plan appealed to the neo-classical period by its geometrical purity. It was also well adapted to Anglican church design at a time when the sermon was all-important.

An original and distinguished design and an uncommonly beautiful position, open entirely towards The Quarry and the river. Yet it is from that very side that one may find a flaw in the no doubt very thoughtful composition. The principal parts of the design are the west tower, as the main external accent, and the circular nave as the internal climax. Seen from the west (i.e. the ritual north), these two parts will not merge. Steuart has avoided that untidy merging which mars so many Georgian churches and which cannot be avoided if the tower seems to stand on the pediment of the nave. But he has gone just a little too far in the logical separation of the two parts. He interpolates an anteroom of square shape with two apses, a room extremely effective inside, but a little troublesome outside. The building material is Grinshill stone of a pale mauve tone.

The interior is a remarkable spatial experience. Three stages – a circular hall under the tower, the anteroom with the two apsed ends in which most elegantly two arms of a staircase sweep up to the gallery, their handrail being of thin simple iron shapes, and the nave or rotunda with its gallery three-quarters round, converting the circular room into a horseshoe auditorium and a separate chancel. The chancel is singled out by pairs of giant Corinthian columns placed behind one another and by a very large Venetian window. The gallery rests on short unfluted Ionic columns, and on these stand exceedingly attenuated Corinthian columns to support the flat ceiling. The columns are of cast iron. Sparing decoration. Very simple pews.
[SHROPSHIRE]

160

69] Tyringham House, Buckinghamshire
Gateway, 1797 by John Soane

Soane, the most original architect of his generation, was inspired by a search for primitive simplicity, one of the mainsprings of European neo-classicism.

Built in 1793–7 for William Praed, banker and entrepreneur, Tyringham was Soane's first mature work. Only the gateway remains unaltered. This is, in spite of its small scale, a monument of European importance. It is a screen of the same kind as Adam's at Syon House or the Hyde Park Corner screen. What is so remarkable about it is that it is entirely independent of period precedent, a sign of a daring only matched at that moment by what Ledoux was designing in France and Gilly in Germany. The Tyringham gateway, which is built of elephant-grey stone, is in addition an extremely exacting piece of design, with emphatically nothing of the elegance of Holland and Wyatt. It consists of a segmental arch on heavy, square, completely unmoulded pillars. The arch is carved out of a big, massive slab, again unmoulded. On top of this is a thin slab, slightly thicker in the centre. The segmental arch is coffered inside, and a band of incised lines marks its edge. Another such band of lines runs along the place on the pillars where one would expect a capital or an abacus, and then runs on across a connecting link to the left and right which has a blank niche and ends at the two end pavilions of the screen composition. These have Tuscan columns *in antis* (with hardly any entasis), the only detail for which a precedent existed. Soane had been in Rome in 1778–9, but such Tuscan columns were more a recent French than an ancient Roman motif.

[BUCKINGHAMSHIRE]

Post-Reformation Monuments

Much of the best English sculpture can be found in cathedrals and churches. The expression of human affection, the commemoration of great deeds, and the belief in an after-life were all powerful motives for erecting funerary monuments and challenged the imagination of sculptors, until in the early nineteenth century the fashion sharply waned.

70] Holy Cross, Felsted, Essex
Monument to the first Lord Rich, died 1568, and his son, died 1581, erected *c.* 1620 by Epiphanius Evesham

Elizabethan and Jacobean monuments celebrate the virtues of those commemorated by symbolism and emblematic means.

The monument, erected probably only about 1620, is attributed convincingly to Epiphanius Evesham. Lord Rich, great-grandson of a London mercer and born in 1496 in the City of London, had risen, by means of ability and absence of scruples, to be made Lord Chancellor in 1548. Big standing wall-monument with the figure of Lord Rich comfortably reclining and looking back at his son, who is kneeling on the ground by the side facing a prayer-desk attached by a generous scroll to the monument. Behind the figure two coats of arms and three reliefs of groups of standing figures, with all the lyrical intensity of which Evesham was capable. They represent Lord Rich with Fortitude and Justice, Lord Rich with Hope and Charity, and Lord Rich with Truth (?) and Wisdom. One looks in vain for Lord Rich with Intolerance and Occasio. The monument is flanked by two tall bronze columns carrying a pediment.
[ESSEX]

71] St Michael, Withyham, East Sussex
Monument to Thomas Sackville, 1677 by Caius Gabriel Cibber

During the seventeenth century dynastic considerations became less overriding in the com-memoration of the dead, and monuments to young wives and to children can be found.

The Sackville Chapel is what matters in the church. The monument for which the chapel was erected is that of Thomas Sackville, who died in 1677 at the age of thirteen. The monument was commissioned in 1677. It is by C. G. Cibber, who was paid £350 for it to be 'artificially performed' and to 'ye well liking of Mr Peter Lilly, his majesty's painter'. Cibber has indeed produced a monument different from any seen in England up to that time, inspired clearly by the Italian Baroque though perhaps by way of Holland.

The monument is placed free standing in the middle of the chapel and is of the traditional tomb-chest type. The material is white and grey marble. The boy reclines on a half-rolled-up mat, definitely a Netherlandish and Elizabetho-Jacobean motif, and holds a skull, and his parents, the fifth Earl and Countess of Dorset, kneel life-size on cushions placed on the steps of the tomb-chest. They look at him disconsolately. As if they had only that moment decided to kneel there, their figures make part of the representations of other children invisible which are placed against the side of the tomb-chest, again a traditional motif. These children kneel or lie in a variety of poses, some holding skulls. The whole has a directness of feeling and expression unprecedented in England.

[SUSSEX]

STAND NOT AMAZ'D READER THO YET IS SHEAD
FROM DEANED EYES VAINE OFFERINGS TO THE DEAD
FOR HE WHOSE SACRED ASHES HEERE DOTH LYE
WAS THE GRAT HONOR OF ALL OVR FAMILY
TO BLAZE SO HONOURD YOVTH IS HVT TO RETRACT
FROM THE MORE THEN NONE CAN SE EXACT
SO GRAVE AND HOPFVL WAS HIS YOVTH
SO DEARE BEYOND TO PIETY AND TRVTH
HE SACRENCE WAS BVT WHAT GREAT NATVRE GAVE
AND YET GRIM DEATH HATH SNATCH'D HIM TO THIS GRAVE
HE NEVER TO HIS PARENTS WAS VNKIND
BVT IN HIS EARLY LEAVING THEM BEHIND
AND SINCE HATH LEFT VS AND FOR EVER GON
WHAT MOTHER WOVLD NOT WEEP FOR SVCH A SON
MAY THIS FAIRE MONVMENT THEN NEVER FADE
OR BY BLASTING TIME OR AGE DECAY'D
THAT THE SVCEEDING TIMES TO ALL MAY TELL
HEERE LIETH ONE THAT LIV'D AND DIED WELL
HEERE LYES THE THIRTEENTH CHILD AND SEVENTH SON
WHO IN HIS THIRTEENTH YEARE HIS RACE HAD RVN.

THOMAS SACKUILLE

72] Westminster Abbey, London
Monument to John, Duke of Argyll and Greenwich,
1748–9 by Louis-François Roubiliac

Roubiliac's monuments, especially those in Westminster Abbey, in their originality and technical
mastery established a new standard in English sculpture.

Nowhere in Westminster Abbey does Roubiliac appear greater as a sculptor. The conceits of the
Nightingale and Hargrave monuments may be more ingenious, but in spirited portraiture and
delicacy of draperies the Argyll monument is supreme and need indeed not fear comparison with
any contemporary monument in France or Italy. The source of the composition is clearly Italy.
Big black base with relief of Liberty with the Phrygian cap and Magna Carta and putti against a
background of lightly indicated architecture. To the left Eloquence standing and looking and
gesticulating towards us; to the right Minerva seated and looking up to the main group. The
figures establish at once the diagonal movement so essential for Baroque composition. Above, on
the sarcophagus, semi-reclining, the Duke, his head to the right, carrying on the movement from
below. His elbow rests on the thigh of Fame standing to the right and writing his name and titles
on an obelisk at the back of the composition. She stops short at the Gr of Greenwich to indicate
that the title died out with him. The obelisk with the figure of Fame writing was taken by
Roubiliac from the Mitrovitz monument at Prague, dated 1714. This was designed by Fischer von
Erlach and is illustrated in his *Historische Architektur* of which an English edition came out in
1730.
[LONDON I : THE CITIES OF LONDON AND WESTMINSTER]

73] Winchester Cathedral, Hampshire
Monument to Joseph Warton, Headmaster of Winchester College,
1801 by John Flaxman

Austere but subtly evocative, this catches the spirit of the reliefs on antique gravestones.

White marble. Warton is seated and looks benign but searching. In front of him four eager and
pretty boys. At the back Aristotle in precise profile, Homer precisely frontal – as neat as Piero
della Francesca. It is one of Flaxman's most successful funerary monuments, intimate yet
monumental. Against the sides two medallions. On the top acroteria and a lyre growing out of
acanthus.

[HAMPSHIRE AND THE ISLE OF WIGHT]

170

74] St George's Chapel, Windsor, Berkshire
Monument to Princess Charlotte, died 1817,
1820–4 by Matthew Cotes Wyatt

Princess Charlotte was the only child of the Prince Regent and his wife, Caroline of Brunswick. The princess's death in childbirth caused great public distress.

If proof were needed that the Romantic decades could combine the sensational with the chaste – here it is. A snow-white scene acted by life-size figures. Below, the princess dead on a ledge covered entirely by a heavy sheet from under which only the fingers of one hand hang down. To the left and right four mourning women, all completely hidden by their mantles. Above, the princess ascending to heaven, one breast bare, and two angels left and right, one holding the still-born baby, the other crossing his arms. All this takes place in front of a stone tomb, the entrance to which is scarcely visible because of a large white curtain. The monument is perhaps the most complete statement of one ideal of funerary sculpture of the early nineteenth century. The effects are very strong, but the whiteness and the emotionless faces that are seen make it safe in the church. The folds also are disturbed only in a few places.
[BERKSHIRE]

The Picturesque:
1800–1850

Richard Payne Knight and Uvedale Price, by their writings on aesthetics and the Picturesque published in the 1790s, codified a new visual awareness. This gave a new lease of life to landscape gardening; it also revolutionized architectural design by making irregularity appear no longer a fault but potentially a virtue. This new insight also stimulated the developing appreciation of Gothic.

75] New River Head, Great Amwell, Hertfordshire
1800 by Robert Mylne

Here is an Arcadian vision inspired by the paintings of Poussin rather than a strictly Picturesque landscape.

The space north of the church is one of the most delightful spots in Hertfordshire, thanks to Robert Mylne, architect to the New River Company and a man eager to perpetuate his own and others' fame. The New River was begun by Sir Hugh Myddelton in 1609 to give London better water. He completed the great enterprise after only four years in 1613. To commemorate this great feat, which was indeed after two hundred years still of some importance to London, Robert Mylne erected a monument to Myddelton, an urn of Coade stone on a pedestal on which we read in pretty letters: 'From the Spring at Chadwell 2 miles west and from this source of Amwell the Aqueduct meanders for the space of XL miles conveying health, pleasure, and convenience to the metropolis of Great Britain . . . an immortal work since man cannot more nearly imitate the Deity than by bestowing health.' Then it goes on to say that the monument was dedicated by 'Robert Mylne, Architect, Engineer etc. in 1800'. It stands on an island in the New River with four weeping willows and a yew tree and smoothly cut lawn. Close to it is the source, also embellished by a stone with a poem:

> O'erhung with shrubs, that fringe the chalky rock
> A little fount pour'd forth its gurgling rill . . .

and another yet smaller island has a second monument to Myddelton, dated 1818:

> AMWELL, perpetual be thy stream
> Nor e'er thy spring be less
> Which thousands drink who never dream
> Whence flow the streams they bless.

[HERTFORDSHIRE]

76] Blaise Hamlet, near Bristol, Avon
1810–11 by John Nash

This captures all the qualities associated with Picturesque beauty – roughness, irregularity, and sudden variation – which Nash and his partner, the landscape gardener Humphry Repton, had aimed for on a larger scale in landscaped parks.

In 1810 John Scandrett Harford, the Quaker banker, asked John Nash to design some estate cottages for old retainers. The result is Blaise Hamlet. This group of detached cottages is the *nec plus ultra* of Picturesque layout and design. English theory about 1800 had preached variety. Here is variety at its most varied. The cottages are grouped along the curving sides of a kind of fairy village green, that is an undulating piece of lawn with a shaft with lantern-head in a place emphatically not central, with a few scattered trees, and with the green running up close to the houses. Each house differs completely from any other – except that they are all of rubble; for the smoothness of brick had to be avoided at all cost. But otherwise there are round chimneys and polygonal chimneys, and diagonally placed chimneys. If they are all top-heavy, that is due to the desire for a picturesque skyline. Then there are pantile roofs and stone slates and of course thatch. The cottage with the thatched front dormer is on the whole the favourite with today's visitors. Blaise Hamlet is indeed responsible for some of the worst sentimentalities of England. Its progeny is legion and includes Christmas cards and teapots. Why then are we not irritated but enchanted by it? I suggest that its saving graces are its smallness, its seclusion from traffic and commerce, and the nicely maintained degree of artificiality throughout.

[NORTH SOMERSET AND BRISTOL]

176

77] Peckforton Castle, Cheshire
c. 1844–50 by Anthony Salvin

Early-nineteenth-century medievalism, fed by numerous antiquarian publications, achieved some highly convincing effects.

Peckforton Castle was built about 1844–50 by Salvin for the first Lord Tollemache. His riches were his estates. The family (in 1883) owned 35,726 acres producing £43,345 annually. Peckforton Castle cost £60,000. *The Illustrated London News* in 1851 said that it 'seems to exhibit the peculiar beauties of Carnarvon Castle without its inconveniences', but Sir George Gilbert Scott, younger than Salvin by a crucial twelve years, obviously referred to Peckforton when in 1858 he called 'the largest and most carefully and learnedly executed Gothic mansion of the present' 'the very height of masquerading'.

So we must see for ourselves. Peckforton is indeed the only fully deceptive of all the English nineteenth-century castles, not just generally medieval and with windows clearly of the nineteenth century as at Smirke's Lowther in Cumbria and Eastnor in Herefordshire and Hopper's Penrhyn in Gwynedd, but a real castle in a position which might have been chosen by any medieval *ingenerius*. It also faces the medieval castle of Beeston in the most challenging way. The approach is romantic, by an asymmetrically composed outer gatehouse with a round turret, and through the wood whose trees are of course now higher than they were meant to be in proportion to the castle.

[CHESHIRE]

Early Victorian Churches

Catholic Emancipation at the end of the 1820s, followed by the Tractarian renewal of the Church of England in the following two decades, promoted an outburst of church building of high architectural ambition which was sustained at a remarkable level until the end of the century.

78] St Mary, Andover, Hampshire
1840–6 by Augustus F. Livesay

This early example of the serious revival of the Early English style for church architecture takes its inspiration from Salisbury Cathedral.

Built at the expense of Dr Goddard, who retired from the headmastership of Winchester College in 1809 to live at Andover. He died in 1845, aged eighty-eight, just before his church had been completed. It is a very remarkable building, and one which for several reasons strikes one as possibly designed or conceived or outlined by the client himself. It was begun in 1840, opened in 1844, and completed, including the tower, in 1846. Goddard's architect was Augustus F. Livesay of Portsmouth, the architect of Holy Trinity at Trowbridge, Wiltshire. However, the building turned out to be structurally unsafe, and so it was handed over to Sydney Smirke. One would like to know more of the early vicissitudes of this extraordinary and really quite brilliant design. The building is consistently Early English, which was not what was fashionable in 1840, though it had been done by Edward Garbett at Theale in Berkshire as early as 1820. Garbett went to Salisbury for inspiration. So did Dr Goddard.

The interior is sensational. Very high nave with a plaster rib-vault. Tall piers with six attached shafts with shaft-rings and moulded capitals. The tower arch is high, but below is a strainer arch, its lower part a normal arch, its upper part curving upward. The east end of the nave is higher than the apse appears inside and has a stepped five-light window leading into the space behind the upper apse windows. The transepts are only as high as the aisles. Transepts and aisles have rib-vaults as well. The wall shafts of aisles and transepts start from twisted or knotted corbels. The apse – a stroke of genius – is separated from the rest of the church by a screen of three arches on immensely long round shafts. The apse itself has double tracery, i.e. tracery in two layers, the climax of this ingenious and fervent design.
[HAMPSHIRE AND THE ISLE OF WIGHT]

79] St Giles, Cheadle, Staffordshire
1841–6 by A. W. N. Pugin

Pugin's best buildings – like this Roman Catholic church – have real quality. His importance, though, was as a polemicist, and his thesis that Gothic was the right style for all sorts of nineteenth-century buildings dominated the architecture of the mid-Victorian decades.

Cheadle is Pugin-land. The Anglican parish church may be quite a substantial building, but what haunts you for miles around is the raised forefinger of Pugin's steeple pointing heavenward. Cheadle, Pugin wrote, is 'a perfect revival of an English parish church of the time of Edward I'. He said so not to praise himself but to praise the Earl of Shrewsbury, at whose expense the church was built. Only here and at St Augustine in Ramsgate, Kent, where he paid himself, was he free of financial stringency. St Augustine is simple and solid and antiquarianly correct – no more; Cheadle is decorated wherever decoration could find a place. But then Pugin was an affluent man, Lord Shrewsbury a very rich man. The Cheadle steeple is one of the most perfect pieces of nineteenth-century Gothic Revival anywhere, especially the sharp spire with two sets of pinnacles. The style is Decorated, and Pugin uses that style throughout the church.

[STAFFORDSHIRE]

80] St Paul, Prior Park, Bath, Avon
1844 by J. J. Scoles, completed after 1863

Built for Roman Catholic worship after the Palladian mansion had been taken over as a boarding school, St Paul represents the classicism which non-Puginian Catholics favoured throughout the nineteenth century.

The interior is immensely impressive, without any doubt the most impressive church interior of its date in the county. Nave and aisles separated by eight fluted Corinthian giant columns on each side carrying not arches but a straight entablature which runs from west to east without any break or projections and recessions. Coffered tunnel-vault with penetrations from the almost invisible clerestory windows. Tall apse with attached columns. The type comes from France and the later eighteenth century (e.g. Chalgrin's Saint-Philippe-du-Roule in Paris, begun in 1774).
[NORTH SOMERSET AND BRISTOL]

High Victorian:
1850–1885

The economic self-confidence of the mid-Victorian period, combined with its moral earnestness, conditioned the character of the architecture of the period, which was one of extreme stylistic variety. Pugin and the critic John Ruskin inspired the seriousness and striving for authenticity which excite respect for High Victorian Gothic even at its most visually overpowering. The classicism of the period tends, by contrast, to be loose and florid.

81] Town Hall, Leeds, West Yorkshire
1853–8 by Cuthbert Brodrick

The developing industrial cities of the Midlands and the North expressed their civic pride in a series of magnificent public halls, some classical, some Gothic.

Leeds can be proud of its town hall, one of the most convincing buildings of its date in the country, and of the classical buildings of its date no doubt the most successful. It was an ambitious thing for the citizens of Leeds to erect a town hall on this scale, but Birmingham and Liverpool had blazed the trail. Leeds came fifteen years later, and hence the ties with the classical past are looser, the Baroque is nearer than the Grecian precedent. The whole façade is giant columns or pilasters, and even the sides do not relax that high rhetoric. Heavily rusticated base. A wide staircase flanked by lions leads up to the central portico of ten giant Corinthian columns. Three-bay pavilions left and right with attached columns between coupled pilasters and arched windows in two storeys. No pediments anywhere. A heavy attic, and over the centre a proud tower 225 ft high, with a detached square colonnade of six columns to each side and a big, tall, rather elongated domical top with concave sides. The architect has not quite made up his mind whether he wanted a dome like those of the Greenwich Hospital or a tower. In the first designs no tower was visualized at all.
[YORKSHIRE: THE WEST RIDING]

82] St Margaret, Leiston, Suffolk
1853 by Edward Buckton Lamb

Mid-Victorian 'rogue' Gothic was associated particularly with the work of certain Low Church architects, who were still designing primarily for good acoustics.

As undauntedly and frantically original as this remarkable architect's other churches. His building is Decorated outside, flint with horizontal stone bands. Nothing prepares us for the antics of carpentry inside. The stone walls are as low as possible so as to get as much space as possible for the timber roof. The church has transepts, and the climax of the design is the crossing, marked by four long and strong diagonal beams rising to the apex and four more diagonals rising a little less so as to come to a point a good deal below the apex. They are connected with the higher quadruplet by diagonal struts.
[SUFFOLK]

188

83] Wellington College, Berkshire
1856–9 by John Shaw Junior

Monumental school building was an expression of Victorian concern for the improvement of educational and moral standards. The lively outline of Wellington is still clearly influenced by the Picturesque.

Wellington College was founded in 1853 as a national memorial to the Duke, who had died in 1852. It was to be a school for orphans of officers, and all the money was voluntarily subscribed. Fees should range from £10 to £20 per annum. The foundation stone was laid in 1856, the school was opened in 1859. The first headmaster, Edward White Benson, ended as Archbishop of Canterbury. The architect, John Shaw, is by and large unknown, though Wellington College alone ought to have secured a lasting reputation for him. He was over fifty when he was recommended for the job by William Burn, the architect, and commissioned. Burn knew Shaw's Royal Naval School at Deptford, London, now Goldsmiths' College, begun in 1843, which is in itself as remarkable a job as Wellington College: an extremely restrained, decidedly Italian design, with a giant middle portal as its only decoration. Commercial buildings by him are fussy and undistinguished. Wellington College is distinguished, it is not at all restrained, and some people may well call it fussy too. However that may be, for the history of Victorian architecture it is highly important; for it is in a style made up of Christopher Wren's Hampton Court and Louis XIII, and that mixture, purged of all fussiness, was going to be reintroduced by Nesfield at Kinmel Park in Clwyd some ten or twelve years later and to start the so-called Queen Anne fashion.

Wren, according to *The Builder* (1, 1843, 218), had interested Shaw already in his early days. It is remarkable that *The Builder* recognized Wren in Shaw; for *The Times* in 1859 called Wellington College 'a handsome edifice in the decorated Italian manner or mixed style'. *The Times* also liked its 'ruddy, cheerful glow'. Cheerful one may well call it, remembering the grim Gothic starkness of contemporary public schools. But the remarkable thing is that Wellington College, in spite of *The Times*, is just not Italianate in the sense of the 1850s nor the purer Cinquecento of Barry in 1850 (Cliveden).

We must now try to define the motifs which Shaw chose and connect them with the general picture of the style of the college. The mansard roofs of course are French, and the window surrounds on the main floor of the east and west ranges with their busy rhythm of brick trim are Louis XIII too. Also such things as the tower tops may have been intended to suggest France. On the other hand the hipped roofs of the other ranges, the segment-headed windows, the main portal (cf. Trinity Library, Cambridge), and the dormers are William and Mary, and the arches of the cloisters are just Victorian and nothing else.

[BERKSHIRE]

84] All Saints, Denstone, Staffordshire
1860–2 by George Edmund Street

This church represents High Victorian originality at its most controlled. Street was deeply learned in medieval architecture, but prided himself that every detail of his buildings was invented, not copied.

Built for Sir Thomas Percival Heywood of the Manchester banking and church-building family. His architect was Street, and here indeed is young Street at his very best – young Street, for he was thirty-six when he designed Denstone in 1860. The building, consecrated in 1862, is in the Middle Pointed, the style of the later thirteenth and early fourteenth centuries, the style Street – like Scott and like the Ecclesiologists – believed to be the best Gothic, but it is highly original in the handling, and it is not provocative, as Butterfield liked to be. Street's elements are the simplest: nave, chancel and rounded apse, north tower. But watch what he does with these elements. The apse e.g. has large windows with plate tracery – Street always preferred the flatter and more solid plate tracery to the wirier and more elegant bar tracery – and massive buttresses, but the buttresses stop at the sill level of the windows. The main windows altogether have plate tracery. In the nave south wall there are three, widely spaced, and of differing patterns. Their arches have alternating cream- and rose-coloured voussoirs, and the walls also have rose bands – the kind of polychromy Butterfield was carrying to extremes. In the chancel Street breaks the order of the windows and suddenly inserts (for inner reasons) two small quatrefoils high up instead of a proper window. On the north side there are only small single lights except for one large quatrefoil which gives light to the font. On the north side also is the tower, and it is round with a conical top, but grows out of an oblong base zone, the vestry, and is reached by an outer stair. This is the one place where the design strikes one as clever rather than organic.
[STAFFORDSHIRE]

85] Town Hall, Manchester
1868–72 by Alfred Waterhouse

Among the High Victorian Gothicists the Quaker Waterhouse designed few churches, but his planning skills gained him a long line of commissions for major public buildings, where the ample circulation areas considered necessary provided scope for the theatrical handling of space.

In 1867 George Godwin, editor of *The Builder*, was asked to inspect the designs which would be sent in for the new town hall to be built at Manchester. 136 were received, and Godwin set aside ten designs by eight architects. They were then passed on to Professor Donaldson and to Street, and the result was that Speakman & Charlesworth of Manchester came first, J. Oldrid Scott second, Thomas Worthington third, and Alfred Waterhouse fourth. Waterhouse was however specially commended for convenience of plan and economic soundness, and so, in the end, he was commissioned. In 1868, when building began, he was thirty-eight years old. The town hall is built of brick with stone facing. The style chosen is Early English.

One enters and finds oneself in a low, vaulted entrance hall and proceeds into another lying across and being three-naved. From this the two staircases rise. The right part of the front next to the tower is the statuary hall, again vaulted in three vessels. The intermediate landing of the staircases has a quadrant-curved wall. Behind the staircases are less ceremonial but visually more thrilling spiral stairs in open shafted cages.

[SOUTH LANCASHIRE]

194

86] Cragside, Rothbury, Northumberland
1870–5 and later by Richard Norman Shaw

Shaw, the most brilliant domestic designer of his generation, took a leading part in the shift from
High Victorian vigour to the subtler and more truly domestic effects of the 1880s and 90s.

The mansion was built in 1870 by Norman Shaw for the first Lord Armstrong, and a wing was added in 1883–5. It is the centre of an estate of 14,000 acres, and the position chosen is one of high romantic glamour, with the Coquet river far down below and woods everywhere. Not another house is visible in any direction. The site is Wagnerian and so is here Shaw's architecture. It has none yet of the finesse of his Chelsea houses of a few years later. Its origin is the Tudor style both in its stone and its black-and-white versions. The Northumbrian hills are not a black-and-white region, but that did not worry Shaw in 1870. What he was concerned with was high picturesqueness for his design, and he has without doubt achieved it. He is said to have made the sketches for the house in one day. The main front which faces the river is a complicated composition of forward and backward and higher and lower elements, though the general impression is one of towering height everywhere.
[NORTHUMBERLAND]

87] Rugby School, Warwickshire
Chapel, 1872 by William Butterfield

Polychromatic brickwork and stonework, inspired by the writings of Ruskin, contributed to some of the strongest effects of High Victorian Gothic. Butterfield was the leading exponent.

The real spirit of Rugger is Butterfield, who was called in in 1859 and commissioned in 1867 to design New Quad. Its south side is formed by the chapel. This is of 1872 and amazingly resourceful. The polychromy is as pronounced as in the rest of the quad, of red and yellow and black brick, with fleuron friezes. The climax of the composition is the octagonal central tower with steep pyramid roof and big gargoyles sparring out. Big broaches mediate between square and octagon. Angular also the polygonal apse. The whole is as multiform and as stepped as possible. To the sides three bays project transeptally, one slightly, the others more boldly and with steep cross gables. That leaves little length to the nave and the very low aisles.
[WARWICKSHIRE]

88] St Agnes, Sefton Park, Liverpool, Merseyside
1883–5 by John Loughborough Pearson

Pearson's vaulted interiors represent the purest ideal of a proper setting for High Anglican ritualistic worship.

St Agnes was built at the expense of Douglas Horsfall, a wealthy stockbroker, who was a benefactor of churches and member of a family of benefactors of churches. The architect of St Agnes was Pearson, and the dates are 1883–5. It is the noblest Victorian church in Liverpool, erect and vigorous, and not in the least humbled by being of red brick. The style is that of the thirteenth century, English with French touches, combined to achieve perfect unity. This was of course Pearson's favourite style, and he knew how to handle it with ease and without ever stooping to imitation.

The interior is ashlar-faced and stone-vaulted, with the quadripartite rib-vaults of French cathedrals. Pearson uses no gallery, but a balcony all along, with the high single lancets of the clerestory above it. The west bay has a tripartite arcade to mark a lobby space. The nave is of four bays. At the east end Pearson intensified his effects by subsidiary structures, low and themselves vaulted. An octagon in the north-east transept with mid-pier to carry the organ, a Lady Chapel off the south-east transept with its own aisles, and the north aisle continued to form a very narrow ambulatory round the apse.

[SOUTH LANCASHIRE]

Arts and Crafts:
1885–1900

Ruskin's writings remained important, but the ideas and achievements of William Morris provided the principal source of inspiration. Architects showed a new respect for the handiwork of the craftsman and for the intrinsic qualities of materials. Many, reacting against High Victorian aggressiveness and trying to catch what they thought was the spirit of Gothic rather than its outward appearance, deliberately aimed at understatement. This was a moment of real originality, when Britain had something to teach the Continent.

89] Holy Trinity, Bothenhampton, Dorset
1887–9 by Edward Schroeder Prior

The office of Norman Shaw trained a series of highly talented architects, most of whom were associated with the Arts and Crafts movement. Prior was perhaps the most original of them all.

Externally nothing special. All the more impressive is the interior. The outside is just nave with bellcote over its east gable, and chancel, rock-faced, with lancet windows. The south porch has sides with trefoil windows in very deep inner reveals. This is an ouverture to the interior. Here Prior did already what he was going to do over fifteen years later at Roker in County Durham, namely to articulate the nave by three sweeping single-chamfered transverse arches. The idea probably came from Norman Shaw's Adcote in Shropshire of 1877. The chancel has the same motif, but here in terms of steep arched braces. Moreover, the chancel windows, including the sedilia, are in excessively deep reveals, and above, just below the springing of the roof and on each side of the chancel, six corbels carry blank arches with the same deep reveals. The church ought to be known much more widely.
[DORSET]

90] Avon Tyrrell, near Ringwood, Hampshire
Hall chimneypiece, 1891 by William Richard Lethaby

Arts and Crafts architects and decorative artists delighted in using materials whose intrinsic beauty required no embellishment.

Built for Lord Manners by Lethaby in 1891. It was his first job, and the job had been offered to Norman Shaw, whose chief assistant and, as Muthesius, an intelligent contemporary, wrote, undoubtedly best pupil he was. Shaw secured the job for young Lethaby, and the result is one of the finest houses of the date in England, Shaw-school, yet already very personal, and subtle and sensitive in the details.

The masterpiece of the interior is the chimneypiece in the principal room. This has no historic connotation any longer. It is basically a chequer of grey and black Derbyshire marble with masses of fossils, but the pattern is much more complex than just a chequer.
[HAMPSHIRE AND THE ISLE OF WIGHT]

91] College of Technology, Romford Road, West Ham, Newham, London
Library and museum, 1896–8 by Gibson & Russell

The 'Queen Anne' of the 1870s and 80s, a fusion of Victorian Gothic ideals with the brick style of the mid seventeenth century, burgeoned at the end of the century into a free Baroque, especially popular for public buildings.

Every conceivable motif is used which was available at that peculiar moment in the history of English architecture when the allegiance to forms of the past was at last thrown to the winds. Giant columns and Gibbs surrounds of windows are still permitted, but the turret and cupola shapes for instance are without any period precedent. Besides, the grouping of masses is completely free. The college front is towards Romford Road, a symmetrical composition with two flanking turrets. The museum projects on the right, a lower domed block, and towards Water Lane the library recedes, ending in a turret of odd and playful shape. Altogether the architects have certainly enjoyed being fanciful and have not minded being a little vulgar. But the whole is of a robust vitality which seems enviable today.

[ESSEX]

206

92] Broadleys (above) and Moor Crag (right), Cartmel Fell, Cumbria 1898–1900 by Charles F. Annesley Voysey

Voysey was single minded in reducing the domestic idiom of the Victorian Gothic architects to a set of symbols for homeliness.

On Windermere and immediately south of the Westmorland boundary are two of Voysey's best houses, Broadleys, on the lake side of the road, and Moor Crag, a little further south, on the other side. They date from 1898–1900, Voysey's years of greatest success and fertility, and there is nothing of the date on the Continent to come up to their standard. The future and the past blend effortlessly indeed. They are twentieth-century pioneer work and yet free Tudor. Their language is unmistakable, and yet they are very different one from the other. Voysey's language means pebbledash, low mullioned windows with completely unmoulded members, iron brackets under the eaves, battered buttresses, and a less analysable sense of comfort and of things falling easily into place. Broadleys has a front to the lake more formal than anything at Moor Crag, and yet not in a set symmetry. The front has three semicircular bow-windows, the left and the middle ones with two transoms, the right one representing two storeys and expressing them. And there is some bare wall to its right which is not matched on the left. Moor Crag has greater emphasis on big sheltering gables. They appear on both main sides and again without formal correspondences.

[NORTH LANCASHIRE]

Edwardian:
1901–1914

The Edwardian age was a transitional period before the sharp break of the First World War. Arts and Crafts ideas persisted, but there was also a strong classical revival. In one or two buildings a premonition of the new century's own idiom can be felt.

93] Luton Hoo, Bedfordshire
Staircase, 1903 by Charles Mewès of Mewès & Davis

Direct French inspiration, rare in England, is here found in a Frenchman's remodelling of one of Robert Adam's grandest houses.

The thrill of the house as it now stands is provided by Mewès of Mewès & Davis, who remodelled it in 1903 for Sir Julius Wernher, diamond magnate in the heroic years of the diamond and gold discoveries in South Africa. Of his remodelling the *clou* is the oval staircase hall, French Beaux Arts at its most convincing and indeed its most splendid. White walls, the staircase rising in a dashing sweep, its balustrade of massive wrought iron to contrast against the whiteness of the rest. Sculptured groups in niches high up, 'L'Amore degli Angeli' by F. Borgonzoli at the foot. Discreet decoration of the walls and the door surrounds. Oval skylight.

Mewès & Davis were the architects of the Ritz, the former Carlton, and the Waldorf in London. To say that is not a slight on Luton Hoo, but a compliment to the Ritz. The combination of Edwardian riches with an exacting French training brought about interiors – at Luton Hoo as at the Ritz – which are of the very highest quality in their own terms. That they were not the terms of the 'Pioneers', i.e. those that led into the new century and its new style, is neither here nor there. At Luton Hoo display was demanded, and it was provided with a panache of which no one after the First World War would have been capable.

[BEDFORDSHIRE AND THE COUNTY OF HUNTINGDON AND PETERBOROUGH]

94] St Mary the Virgin, Great Warley, Essex
1904 by Charles Harrison Townsend

Architecture and fittings are fused together at Great Warley by symbolism and by the use of exotic materials.

Charles Harrison Townsend was the architect of the Whitechapel Gallery and the Horniman Museum in London. St Mary has a modestly pretty exterior embedded in trees, roughcast *à la* Voysey with buttresses *à la* Voysey and a bell-turret. But the inside is an orgy of the English Arts-and-Crafts variety of the international Art Nouveau. Tunnel-vaulted with broad decorated silver bands across, apse with silver decoration. Panelled walls with lilies in the design. The font with two standing bronze angels, the screen with a wild growth of flowering fruit trees, etc., are all by William Reynolds-Stephens; the stalls and pews were designed less excessively by Townsend himself. The stained glass in the apse windows is by Heywood Sumner.
[ESSEX]

95] Quarr Abbey, Isle of Wight
1911–12 by Dom Paul Bellot

A quite exceptional building in England, Quarr is understandable only in a European context.

In 1907 Quarr House, a Victorian house, was sold to French Benedictines of Solesmes, and in 1908 the new buildings began to rise to its south. They were designed by Dom Paul Bellot, who went on living at Quarr. Later in life he moved to Canada and died there in 1943. He had been born in 1876, the son of an architect, and had studied architecture at the École des Beaux Arts in Paris. He took his diploma in 1900, but decided for a monastic life and was accepted a monk at Solesmes in 1904. He built much in Holland and also in Belgium, France, and Canada, but Quarr is his outstanding achievement. Why does he not appear in all the histories of twentieth-century architecture? Why have those younger scholars not discovered him yet who are looking for a pedigree for 1960 Expressionism by way of 1920 Expressionism? He should appear in books in the line of descent of the early Gaudí of the Casa Vicens and then of Berlage and de Klerk and of Hoeger in Germany. But this attempt at historical placing should not reduce anyone's respect for Bellot's originality and achievement. The church was built in 1911–12. It is built of Belgian bricks, rough, unattractive bricks, bricks others would have tried to hide. It is high and long and high again, and its plan is wholly original. It consists of a short and low nave, then, a few steps up, a long choir with bare side walls, very narrow side passages (like Gaudí's corridors at the college of St Teresa at Barcelona), and ampler galleries above, and then an altar space under a high square tower. Everything is of the same brick, externally and internally.

Paul Bellot was a virtuoso in brick. All is brick and all has to be done angularly; for such is the brick's nature. Instead of pointed arches triangular heads. Stepped gables for the low façade of the church and for the entrance to the abbey, cut-brick friezes and stepped patterns of all kinds. They are again curiously reminiscent of Gaudí. Inside the church, and also the chapter house and the refectory, Paul Bellot repeats one powerful motif: transverse pointed brick arches carrying the roofs, and that is a Catalan motif as well, used in religious and secular architecture and especially similar to Quarr in the Cistercian abbey of Poblet. But it is also present in such south French Cistercian buildings as Le Thoronet. But Spain altogether must have impressed Paul Bellot most; for the tremendous arches inside the east tower of the church, dazzling with the arched openings pierced in the spandrels, are inspired in their crossing – two diagonal ribs and four running from the middle of one side to the middle of the next – by the mosque at Cordova. The way in which the four immensely high narrow windows in the east wall are cut into by the ribs in the tower and the series of open arches in the spandrels are brilliant indeed and establish Dom Paul Bellot beyond doubt as one of the pioneers of twentieth-century Expressionism.
[HAMPSHIRE AND THE ISLE OF WIGHT]

Modern:
1930–1965

The International Modern Style treated planning requirements and the nature of materials as fundamental. It jettisoned the classical tradition, historicist quotation, and even the symbolic use of forms. Of this fundamental reappraisal Adolf Loos and Walter Gropius were the pioneers in Germany, Le Corbusier in France. In England during the 1930s hardly anyone took it seriously, and it was only after the Second World War that this country caught up with the Continent.

96] Marlborough College, Wiltshire
Science Building, 1933 by W. G. Newton

Newton's Memorial Hall at Marlborough, of 1921 (on the left), had been conventionally classical, so the switch of styles for the Science Building is intriguing.

The main extension of the college premises took place west of the main buildings. Here W. G. Newton designed two buildings which, in their stylistic contrast, are most characteristic of the moment when they went up. The Memorial Hall was first designed in 1921 and finally inaugurated in 1925. It is of brick with ample stone dressings. Behind the hall is the other building, the Science Building, in quite a different mood, because dedicated to a different purpose. This was begun in 1933. It is star-shaped with a central lantern. The walls are of concrete, and there are strips of spacious windows. Here was acceptance of the twentieth-century idiom at a moment relatively early as English architectural history goes, and still only with the qualification that what is good enough for stinks is not good enough for prize-givings.
[WILTSHIRE]

97] The Zoo, Dudley, West Midlands
Entrance, 1936–7 by Tecton

Concrete, exploited on the Continent from about 1910 both as exposed structure and for expressive effect, was taken up in England only in the 1930s. Particularly imaginative were the experiments of Tecton, the firm in which Berthold Lubetkin collaborated with a group of young British architects.

Happily mixed up with the outer bailey of the castle. The mixture comes off well, however savagely the Royal Fine Arts Commission, if it were today, would oppose the outrage. After all, medieval castles sometimes had wild beasts in the moat. Only today they are better housed. This is due to Messrs Tecton who did the buildings for the zoo in 1936–7, having made a name by their buildings for the London Zoo, of which the first were designed in 1934. The style of Tecton's zoo buildings is remarkable indeed, even internationally speaking. For it was not the International Modern of the thirties, crisp and clear, rectangular and rational. On the contrary – it indulges in bold curves and their interplay, preparing the ground, as it were, for the fifties and the sixties. This attitude of hostility against what is merely sensible faces you at once. The gates with the five guichets have a number of canopies independent of each other, but interlocked. Each canopy is a shallow horizontally placed S.

[STAFFORDSHIRE]

98] Royal Festival Hall, Lambeth, London
1949–51 by J. Leslie Martin & Robert Matthew

Erected for the Festival of Britain, this was the first major post-war public building in a completely Modern style, without historicist overtones of any kind.

Aesthetically the Festival Hall's greatest achievement, and one which is without doubt internationally remarkable, is the management of inner space. Here, chiefly in the staircases, promenades, superimposed restaurants, etc., are a freedom and intricacy of flow, in their own way as thrilling as what we see in the Baroque churches of Germany and Austria. The various levels are nowhere placed above each other without either ingeniously contrived intermediate stages or without opening into one another by galleries, landings, or some such means. The circuits at stalls and balcony heights for instance are an experience well worth lingering over. Equally delightful is the ascent of the main stairs towards the north, where one reaches a landing from which the angles and bottom corners of the hall are visible and it seems as though the whole huge box of the hall proper were suspended without any support. Altogether if it were not for the fact that the hall is raised to what corresponds to second or third floor level and stands on retracted pillars, nothing like this spatial flux could have been obtained. This ingenious arrangement made it possible to have a large concourse right through the building below the hall. The careful choice of materials and colours also helps, much glass opening out vistas in all directions, divers timbers, slatted or reeded wooden surfaces, grey Derbyshire marble slabs, rendering in various unobtrusive colours, excellently designed carpets and textiles.
[LONDON 2 : EXCEPT THE CITIES OF LONDON AND WESTMINSTER]

99] Coventry Cathedral, West Midlands
Chapel of Gethsemane, 1951–62 by Basil Spence

Coventry Cathedral was the first (and almost the only) building in Britain in a contemporary style to catch the public imagination.

Coventry was raised to cathedral rank in 1918. St Michael, the prime parish church, became the cathedral. On 14 November 1940 it was largely destroyed. A competition for a new building was held in 1951 and won by (Sir) Basil Spence. The principal features of his design had come to him when he first visited the site: the placing north to south and the use of the ruin of the old church as a forecourt. The design, when made known, was blamed by the moderns as not modern enough, by the traditionalists as too modern, by the man in the street as jazzy.

The Chapel of Gethsemane is the smallest in the cathedral. There are only a few benches in it, for intimate devotion, and the feeling is one of being in a cave. On the back wall in ceramics the large, consciously Byzantine angel of Gethsemane and a panel of the sleeping disciples by Steven Sykes. The entrance side is a screen with a large wrought-iron Crown of Thorns designed by Sir Basil himself. So here we are back at the criticism of the furnishings and the building as corny.

What is meant by that? That it appeals to all? For it does; two years after the consecration thousands still go on the pilgrimage and queue outside to be let in. Do they come to pray in the house of God which was bombed and rebuilt? No – they come to admire a work of architecture and works of art. And they are the same who wrote hardly more than twelve years before: 'this unusually ugly factory . . . resembling a cockroach . . . the gasholder on one side and the glorified dustbin on the other . . . an utter monstrosity . . . a concrete disgrace.' These were the people who wanted their cathedrals still imitation-Gothic or imitation-Early-Christian. Could Sir Basil Spence have convinced them so spectacularly in such a short time, if he had not thought from the beginning in terms of a building conducive to worship? Had he been entirely uncompromising, he would not only have had no chance of winning the competition and building the building, he would also have had no chance of winning those for whom he built. And to think of them in the first place surely is true, spiritual, functionalism.

[WARWICKSHIRE]

100] St John's College, Cambridge
Cripps Building, 1963–7 by Philip Powell & J. Hidalgo Moya

Colleges at Oxford and Cambridge have given contemporary architects some of their best opportunities.

The Cripps Building is a masterpiece by one of the best architectural partnerships in the country, both partners mature but still young. They made their name as winners of the competition for housing in Pimlico in 1946 and have since then never produced anything unworthy of them. They entered the academic field with a brilliant piece of infill at Brasenose College in Oxford in 1959–61. For John's they were asked to provide accommodation for 191 undergraduates, 8 fellows' sets, and a Junior Common Room. The site north of New Court and south of Lutyens's brick range of Magdalene made it advisable to build one long range. It is in the articulation of this that Powell & Moya's ingeniousness and sensitivity proved themselves.

The building is of reinforced concrete, faced with Portland stone, and has bronze windows. It is four storeys high and has in addition a number of penthouses. One approaches it in studied meanness through the middle of New Court. The surprise is supreme. The building as first seen forms a turfed court with the dreary back of New Court. The east side is half open to the river. The building only projects that far and turns east to meet the river with its thin end, just enough to make an explicit statement, not enough to prevail over New Court, the Bridge of Sighs, and Lutyens behind the weeping willows at Magdalene. The west side of the court is the one-storeyed Junior Common Room, and one can see at once that the long building carries on from east to west and turns by forty-five degrees in a south-westerly direction. What follows beyond is not revealed. It is a second completely new court, with the new building on the south-west and south-east in axis with the School of Pythagoras at the far north-west end, continued by the new workshop and squash court.

The broken line of this long ribbon of a building is masterly. It is brought home with great intensity by the covered promenade which runs all along, mostly with inhabited space one side, but once – in a strategic position – open to both sides. The broken line creates variety. The unity of the whole composition is, however, expressed in just as masterly a way. This is clearly a series of repeating units, each unit established by the top-hamper of lead-sheathed tank and two penthouses. This roof contraption succeeds splendidly in its scanning function, but in detail it is one of the only two modish features. The canopies of the penthouses are far too bulky, in the way in which the Brutalists like to use their concrete chunks. Still, Powell & Moya, enemies of 'motifs' and of passing fashions, felt probably that very forceful accents were needed. They entirely established a sense of order throughout a building which shuns all excesses. The sense of order expresses itself also in the even size of all the bay-windows, and in the completely even height of all the windows.

[CAMBRIDGESHIRE]

224

101] St Catherine's College, Oxford
1960–4 by Arne Jacobsen

In this decade dominated by the drama and eccentricities of Brutalism, Jacobsen's designs represent the continuation of the austerity and discipline of early International Modern principles.

Here is a perfect piece of architecture. It has a consistent plan, and every detail is meticulously worked out. Self-discipline is its message, expressed in terms of a geometry pervading the whole and the parts and felt wherever one moves or stops. The buildings are one long rectangle, 600 ft long. The major part of the long sides is residential, one range west, one east. Between them, and much broader, and all identical in width, are lecture rooms, library, and hall. An area enclosed by low walls between the lecture rooms and the library contains the tower, the one part not placed axially, because it is a unique part. Between the library and the hall is a lawn, and the lawn is circular (though again one tree has been planted out of axis, because nature is nature). From the hall branch out the Senior Common Rooms to the west, the Junior Common Rooms to the east, identical in area. The geometry is made to tell yet further in the paving of paths through the garden areas inside and outside the parallelepiped, all of the same oblong slabs and never moving in an undulating way, and in the many screen walls, high or low, including those placed fin-wise to demarcate the gardens inside the parallelepiped from the more public circulation areas.

Materials and structure are of the same clarity. Structure is concrete, and frame and beam ends show. The beams which have to do the heaviest carrying are very large, in height only (5 ft), not in width. Infill is brick, a sand-coloured brick of a special two-inch size and used in stretchers only.

And so to the most sweeping criticism that has been made: 'C'est magnifique, mais ce n'est pas un collège.' If a college to be a college must have a variety of moods due to a variety of style and dates of building, then St Catherine's is not a college, nor can any new college be, including Churchill at Cambridge. If a college must have a variety of moods merely due to a variety of sizes and shapes and vistas, then Churchill is and St Catherine's is not. But if a college is a college by having its own distinctive individual mood suited to be the surroundings for young people for their most impressionable years, then St Catherine's is a college. If young people don't like it, that may be an argument against them rather than against the college – always admitting that the Junior Common Rooms are alarming. My final verdict is that the college may have to wait until by the swing of the pendulum of history the ideal of self-permissiveness among students becomes once more the ideal of self-discipline.

[OXFORDSHIRE]

226

Acknowledgements for photographs

Item number

Architect and Building News 97
Architectural Review 98
Austin, James page 6, 2, 3, 10, 15(right), 24, 43, 50, 66, 89, 92(right), 100
Barnes, G. L. 84
Cash, J. Allan 36
Country Life 56, 90, 93
Courtauld Institute of Art, Conway Library 15(left), 70, 88
Dalton, Christopher 13, 26, 54, 67
Donat, John 99
Greeley, Alan 60, 69
Hall, George H. 1, 7, 9, 14, 16, 19, 23, 30, 31(right), 39, 41(right), 47, 51(both), 62(left), 76(right), 80, 81, 87, 96

Howard, Geoff 55
Kersting, A. F. 5, 6, 8, 11, 12, 17(both), 18, 20, 22, 25(right), 27, 28, 31(left), 32, 33, 35, 37, 38, 40, 45, 46, 49, 52, 53(both), 57, 58, 62(right), 63, 64, 65, 71, 72, 73, 76(left), 82, 83, 86, 91
Maré, Eric de 75
Royal Commission on the Historical Monuments of England 42, 44, 59, 68(both), 79, 85
Sanderson & Dixon 92(left)
Smith, Edwin 4, 21, 25(left), 29, 48, 61, 74, 94
Spain, Alan, and Nelson Christmas 77
Taylor, Frank 95
Toomey, W. J. 34
Westwood, Colin 101
Whitaker, Jeremy 41(left), 78

Index

The index consists of the names of buildings, and their architects, which are also the subjects of entries in *The Buildings of England*. Page references to the introduction (which alone has no accompanying illustrations) are in *italic*.

Adam, Robert (1728–92), *21*, 152, 154

Akroyd, John (1556–1613), 118

Andover (Hants), St Mary, 180

Arbury Hall (Warw), dining room, 150

Arup Associates (fl. 1963–), *16*

Avon Tyrrell (Hants), hall chimneypiece, 204

Barnack (Cambs), St John Baptist, relief of Christ in Majesty, 28

Bath (Avon), 41 Gay Street and the Circus, 148; St Paul, Prior Park, 184

Bellot, Dom Paul (1876–1944), 214

Beningbrough Hall (N Yorks), entrance hall, 136

Bentley, John (*c.* 1573–1615), 118

Blaise Hamlet (Avon), 176

Bolton Castle (N Yorks), 94

Bonomi, Joseph (1739–1808), 158

Borgonzoli, F., 210

Boston (Lincs), St Botolph, tower, 78

Bothenhampton (Dorset), Holy Trinity, 202

Boyton (Wilts), St Cosmas and St Damian, south chapel, 60

Bracknell (Berks), Point Royal, *16*

Brinkburn Priory (Northumberland), *20*

Bristol Cathedral (Avon), chapter house, 38; choir aisle, *19*, 66

Broadleys (Cumbria), *see* Cartmel Fell

Brodrick, Cuthbert (1822–1905), 186

Burlington, Richard Boyle, third Earl of (1694–1753), 142

Butley Priory (Suffolk), gatehouse, 72

Butterfield, William (1814–1900), *21*, 198

Caius, Dr John (1510–73), 110

Cambridge (Cambs), Gonville and Caius College, Gate of Virtue, 110; King's College, chapel, *20*, 88; Gibbs Building, *19*; St John's College, Cripps Building, 224; Trinity College, library, 130

Cartmel Fell (Cumbria), Broadleys and Moor Crag, 208

Castle Bolton (N Yorks), *see* Bolton Castle

Castle Howard (N Yorks), mausoleum, 140

Castle Rising (Norfolk), keep, 44

Cheadle (Staffs), St Giles, 182

Chelmsford (Essex), Shire Hall, 156

Chillingham (Northumberland), St Peter, Gray monument, 86

Cibber, Caius Gabriel (1630–1700), 130, 166

Clayton & Bell, 7, 22

Cleator (Cumbria), St Leonard, *10*

Coade, Mrs E., 156, 174

Cold Hanworth (Lincs), All Saints, *14*

Compton Wynyates (Warw), 100

Cottingham, Lewis (1787–1847), 36

Covehithe (Suffolk), St Andrew, *13*

Coventry Cathedral (W Midlands), Chapel of Gethsemane, 222

Cragside (Northumberland), 196

Croft, J., *14*

Denstone (Staffs), All Saints, 192

Dudley Zoo (W Midlands), entrance, 218

Durham Cathedral (Co. Durham), nave, 34

East Knoyle (Wilts), St Mary, plasterwork in the chancel, 126

East Moors (N Yorks), St Mary Magdalene, *16*

Egan, James, *14*

Ely Cathedral (Cambs), Octagon, *19*, 68

Ely, Reginald (fl. 1438–d. 1471), 88

Escomb (Co. Durham), St John the Evangelist, 26

Evesham, Epiphanius (b. 1570), 164

Felsted (Essex), Holy Cross, Rich monument, 164

Ferrey, Benjamin (1810–80), 80

Flaxman, John (1755–1826), 170

Forde Abbey (Dorset), abbot's lodging, 102

Fountains Abbey (N Yorks), 42

Garrett, Daniel (d. 1753), 140

Garton-on-the-Wolds (Humberside), St Michael, 7

Geddington (Northants), Eleanor Cross, 62

Gibbons, Grinling (1648–1721), 122

Gibbs, James (1682–1754), 134

Gibson & Russell (fl. 1890–9), 206

Goddard, Dr W. S. (1757–1845), 180

Great Amwell (Herts), New River Head, 174

Great Packington (Warw), St James, 158

Great Paxton (Cambs), Holy Trinity, crossing, 30

Great Waltham (Essex), Langleys, dining room, 120

Great Warley (Essex), St Mary the Virgin, 212

Great Yarmouth (Norfolk), St Nicholas, *17*

Hall, E. T. & E. S., *17*

Hanbury Hall (Hereford and Worcester), 132

Hardman, John, 22

Hardwick Hall (Derbyshire), 114

Hardwick, Philip (1792–1870), 13

Hare, H. T. (1860–1921), 15–16

Hawksmoor, Nicholas (c. 1661–1736), 15, 18, 21, 140

Hereford Cathedral (Hereford and Worcester), Aquablanca monument and north transept, 58; crossing tower, 12

Hexham Priory (Northumberland), 13

Higham, G., 150

Jackson, Sir Thomas G. (1835–1924), 16

Jacobsen, Arne (d. 1971), 226

Johnson, John (1732–1814), 156

Johnson, John (nineteenth-century), 12

Jones, Inigo (1573–1652), 12, 122

Keene, Henry (1726–76), 150

Kent, William (1685–1748), 144, 146

Kew Palace (The Dutch House) (LB Richmond), 124

Kilpeck (Hereford and Worcester), St Mary and St David, 36

Lamb, Edward Buckton (1806–69), 14, 188

Lambeth (LB Lambeth), Royal Festival Hall, 18, 220

Lastingham (N Yorks), St Mary, crypt, 32

Leeds (W Yorks), Town Hall, 186

Leiston (Suffolk), St Margaret, 188

Lethaby, William Richard (1857–1931), 204

Lewyn, John (fl. 1364–d. c. 1398), 94

Little Maplestead (Essex), St John the Baptist, 20

Little Wenham Hall (Suffolk), 90

Liverpool (Merseyside), St Agnes, Sefton Park, 200

Livesay, Augustus F. (1807–79), 180

London (central; see also Kew, Lambeth, Osterley, West Ham), Berkeley Square (No. 44), staircase, 146; Euston Arch, 13; Foreign Office, 21; Great Marlborough Street, 17; Institute of Chartered Accountants, 18; Law Courts, 21; Queen's Chapel, 122; St Mary-le-Strand, 134; St Stephen Walbrook, 128; Temple Church, choir, 50; Westminster Abbey, Argyll monument, 168

Lubetkin, Berthold (b. 1901), 218

Luton Hoo (Beds), staircase, 210

Madley (Hereford and Worcester), Church of the Nativity of the Virgin, 14

Malmesbury Abbey (Wilts), south porch, 40

Manchester (Greater Manchester), 18; Town Hall, 21, 194; see also Wythenshawe

Marlborough College (Wilts), Memorial Hall and Science Building, 216

Martin, Sir Leslie (b. 1908), and Sir Robert Matthew (1906–75), 220

Mayfield Palace (E Sussex), 92

Mewès, Charles (1860–1914), 210

Moor Crag, see Cartmel Fell

Moore, Temple (1856–1920), 11, 16

Moreton Corbet Castle (Salop), 112

Morris, William (1834–96), 21

Much Marcle (Hereford and Worcester), St Bartholomew, Grandison monument, 76

Much Wenlock Priory (Salop), 10

Mylne, Robert (1733–1811), 174

Nash, John (1752–1835), 176

Needham Market (Suffolk), St John Baptist, roof, 82

Newby Hall (N Yorks), sculpture gallery, 154

Newcastle-under-Lyme (Staffs), Holy Trinity, 14

Newton, W. G. (1885–1949), 216

Norwich (Norfolk), Cathedral, doorway from north walk of cloister, 74; St Peter Mancroft, tower, 15

Orford Castle (Suffolk), keep, 46

Osterley Park House (LB Hounslow), 152

Oxford (Oxon), All Souls College, 22; Clarendon Building, 15; Examination Schools, 16; St Catherine's College, 226; Schools Quadrangle, frontispiece, 118; Town Hall, 15–16

Pace, G. G. (1915–75), 16

Pearson, John Loughborough (1817–97), 21, 200

Peckforton Castle (Ches), 178

Powell & Moya (fl. 1946–   ), 224

Prior, Edward Schroeder (1852–1932), 202

Pugin, A. W. N. (1812–52), 21, 182

Quarr Abbey (IoW), 214

Reynolds-Stephens, William (1862–1943), 212

Rievaulx Terraces (N Yorks), 20

Robinson, Sir Thomas (c. 1702–77), 140

Roubiliac, Louis-François (c. 1705–1762), 168

Rudhall, William (c. 1660–1733), 132

Rufford Old Hall (Lancs), great hall, 98

Rugby School (Warw), chapel, 198

Rushton (Northants), Triangular Lodge, 116

Rushton Spencer (Staffs), St Lawrence, 14

Rysbrack, J. Michael (1694–1770), 144

St Mawes Castle (Cornwall), 104

Salisbury Cathedral (Wilts), Bridport monument, 56; spire, 70

Salvin, Anthony (1799–1881), 178

Scarborough (N Yorks), Grand Hotel, 15

Scheemakers, Peter (1691–1781), 144

Scoles, J. J. (1798–1863), 184

Scott, Sir George Gilbert (1811–78), 21, 80

Seaton Delaval Hall (Northumberland), 138

Shaw, John, the younger (1803–70), 190
Shaw, Richard Norman (1831–1912), 196
Shrewsbury (Salop), St Chad, 160
Skipwith (N Yorks), St Helen, *13*
Sledmere (Humberside), St Mary, *11*
Smirke, Sydney (1797–1877), 180
Soane, Sir John (1753–1837), *21*, 162
Southill (Beds), *14*
South Tidworth (Hants), St Mary, *12*
Spence, Sir Basil (1907–76), 222
Steuart, George (*c.* 1730–1806), 160
Stockton, Thomas, 88
Stourhead (Wilts), *20*
Stowe (Bucks), Temple of British Worthies, 144
Stragglethorpe (Lincs), St Michael, 22
Street, George Edmund (1824–81), *21*, 192
Sumner, Heywood (1853–1940), 212
Swimbridge (Devon), St James, rood screen, 84
Sykes, Steven, 222
Talman, William (1650–1719), 132
Tattershall (Lincs), Holy Trinity, *15*
Taunton (Som), St Mary Magdalene, tower, 80
Tayler & Green (fl. *c.* 1938–*c.* 1959), *17*
Tecton (fl. 1932–48), 218
Thirkleby (N Yorks), All Saints, *14*
Thornhill, Sir James (1675/6–1734), 132
Thornton, William (*c.* 1670–1721), 136
Townsend, Charles Harrison, 212
Tresham, Sir Thomas (1543?–1605), 116
Tynemouth Priory (Tyne and Wear), east end, 48
Tyringham House (Bucks), gateway, 162

Vanbrugh, Sir John (1664–1726), *21*, 138
Voysey, Charles F. Annesley (1857–1941), 22, 208
Warkworth Castle (Northumberland), 96
Wastell, John (fl. 1485–d. 1515?), 88
Waterhouse, Alfred (1830–1905), *21*, 194
Wellington College (Berks), 190
Wells Cathedral (Som), north porch, 52; retrochoir, 64
Westerley, Robert (fl. 1424–61), 88
West Ham (LB Newham), College of Technology,
    library and museum, 206
Westminster, *see* London
West Walton (Norfolk), St Mary, 54
Whitfield, William (b. 1920), *18*
Winchester Cathedral (Hants), Gardiner chantry chapel,
    106; Warton monument, 170
Windsor (Berks), St George's Chapel, monument to
    Princess Charlotte, 172
Wing (Bucks), All Saints, Dormer monument, 108
Winterton (Norfolk), Holy Trinity, *15*
Withyham (E Sussex), St Michael, Sackville monument,
    166
Wood, John, I (1704–54) and II (1728–81), 148
Worcester Cathedral (Hereford and Worcester), choir,
    13
Wren, Sir Christopher (1632–1723), *21*, 128, 130
Wyatt, Matthew Cotes (1777–1862), 172
Wyatt, Sir Matthew Digby (1820–77), 22
Wythenshawe (Gtr Manchester), William Temple
    Memorial Church, *16*
York (N Yorks), Assembly Rooms, 142

The Buildings of England

Founding Editor: Nikolaus Pevsner
Consultant Editor John Newman
Joint Editors: Bridget Cherry and Judy Nairn

By Nikolaus Pevsner, unless otherwise stated.
The dates given are of the first edition (from which quotations are taken),
and of the latest subsequent edition.

Bedfordshire and the County of Huntingdon and Peterborough *1968*

Berkshire *1966*

Buckinghamshire *1960*

Cambridgeshire *1954, revised 1970*

Cheshire *with Hubbard 1971*

Cornwall *1951, revised Radcliffe 1970*

Cumberland and Westmorland *1967*

Derbyshire *1953, revised Williamson 1978*

Devon, North *1952*

Devon, South *1952*

Dorset *with Newman 1972*

Durham *1953, revised Williamson 1983*

Essex *1954, revised Radcliffe 1965*

Gloucestershire: The Cotswolds *Verey, revised 1979*

Gloucestershire: The Vale and the Forest of Dean *Verey 1970, revised 1976*

Hampshire and the Isle of Wight *with Lloyd 1967*

Herefordshire *1963*

Herfordshire *1953, revised Cherry 1977*

Kent, North East and East *Newman 1969, revised 1983*

Kent, West, and Weald *Newman 1969, revised 1976*

Middlesex *1951*

Lancashire, North *1969*

Lancashire, South *1969*

Leicestershire and Rutland *1960, revised Williamson 1985*

Lincolnshire *with Harris 1964*

London 1: The Cities of London and Westminster *1957, revised Cherry 1973*

London 2: Except the Cities of London and Westminster *1952*

London 2: South with Cherry *1983*

Norfolk, North East, and Norwich *1962*

Norfolk, North West and South *1962*

Northamptonshire *1961, revised Cherry 1973*

Northumberland *with Richmond 1957*

Nottinghamshire *1951, revised Williamson 1979*

Oxfordshire *with Sherwood 1974*

Shropshire *1958*

Somerset, North, and Bristol *1958*

Somerset, South and West *1958*

Staffordshire *1974*

Suffolk *1961, revised Radcliffe 1974*

Surrey *with Nairn 1962, revised Cherry 1971*

Sussex *with Nairn 1965*

Warwickshire *with Wedgwood 1966*

Wiltshire *1963, revised Cherry 1975*

Worcestershire *1968*

Yorkshire: North Riding *1966*

Yorkshire: York and the East Riding *with Hutchinson 1972*

Yorkshire: West Riding *1959, revised Radcliffe 1967*